Making Wooden Jigsaw Puzzles

Making Wooden Jigsaw Puzzles

Jigsaw Puzzles

Evan J. Kern

STACKPOLE
BOOKS

Published by
STACKPOLE BOOKS
5067 Ritter Road
Mechanicsburg, PA 17055

Printed in the United States of America

10 9 8 7 6 5 4 3 2 1

FIRST EDITION

Cover design by Kathleen D. Peters
Cover photograph by Evan J. Kern; original photograph of Studley Tool Chest, courtesy of Taunton Press

Library of Congress Cataloging-inPublication Data

Kern, Evan J.
    Making wooden jigsaw puzzles / Evan J. Kern.—1st ed.
       p.   cm.
    Includes bibliographical references.
    ISBN 0-8117-2555-3
    1. Wooden toy making. 2. Jigsaw puzzles. I. Title.
TT174,5,W6K47   1996
745.592—dc20
            96-3963
            CIP

To Lucy

CONTENTS

INTRODUCTION

THE EARLIEST KNOWN WOODEN JIGSAW puzzle dates to 1766, when Englishman John Spilsbury made one called "Europe Divided into Its Kingdoms."[1] Spilsbury glued a map of Europe to a wooden panel and cut along the borders of the countries. This puzzle was an educational tool to teach geography to children and was called a "dissected puzzle." Such puzzles eventually came to be known as jigsaw puzzles, probably with the transition from hand-crafted to machine-cut puzzles in the nineteenth century during the industrial revolution.

These first jigsaw puzzles were cut by hand with a fretsaw, a close relative to the more familiar coping saw, and were made possible by the development of small, inexpensive, replaceable saw blades. Making hand-cut puzzles was very time-consuming, and as a consequence, the puzzles were expensive. With the development of the powered fretsaw, which became known as a jigsaw, the process could be speeded up. These industrial saws were belt driven from line shafts by water wheels, steam engines, and finally, electric

motors. The jigsaw and scroll saw seem to have developed simultaneously.

As the popularity of jigsaw puzzles continued to grow, manufacturers sought means of producing them more economically. One method developed was stack cutting, in which several puzzle boards were fastened together with pins through small holes drilled in the corners of the puzzles. The stack of puzzles would then be cut as if it were one puzzle. For little more effort than was required to cut one puzzle, four to six puzzles could be cut. This economy of effort did not come without sacrifice, however. The considerably larger blade needed to cut a stack of puzzles resulted in pieces that were loose fitting and consequently less desirable for the puzzle enthusiast.

A second and much more far-reaching solution to mass-producing puzzles was the introduction of die cutting. In die cutting, thin, sharp strips of steel known as rules are formed into the shapes of puzzle pieces and are secured to a massive steel plate called a die. The die is fastened into a mechanical press, a puzzle board is placed beneath the die, and the press is closed, forcing the steel rules through the puzzle board and cutting all the puzzle pieces simultaneously. Hundreds of puzzles

---

1. Anne D. Williams, *Jigsaw Puzzles: An Illustrated History and Price Guide* (Radnor, PA: Wallace-Homestead Book Co., 1990), 4.

"Europe Divided into Its Kingdoms" is the earliest known wooden jigsaw puzzle, cut in 1766 by John Spilsbury, an English puzzle maker. It was called a "dissected puzzle" and was made for the purpose of teaching geography. The puzzle is now in a private collection. Photograph by Harry L. Rinker.

can thus be cut in a single day by a single press operator.

Wood was much too hard to be cut with a die, however, and a softer material had to be used. Cardboard die-cut puzzles soon dominated the puzzle market, and by 1975 there were no longer any major jigsaw puzzle manufacturers making wooden puzzles. If not for the efforts of a small number of craftsmen, the tradition of making wooden jigsaw puzzles would have faded into obscurity.

In recent years there have been new attempts to develop mechanical means for commercially producing wooden jigsaw puzzles. Computer programs control the shapes of the pieces being cut, and the puzzle board is cut by forcing water through a precision nozzle under high pressure known as water-jet technology. The stream of water cuts through the wood so rapidly that the wood does not become damp. The quality of the line cut with the jet of water on the picture side of the puzzle board is equal to or better than that achieved with a scroll saw, but as the jet of water travels through the puzzle board, its path gradually widens and produces a ragged edge on the back of the puzzle board. Even should this problem be solved, it is doubtful that water-jet technology will replace hand-cut wooden jigsaw puzzles because most people who buy wooden jigsaw puzzles do so precisely because they are hand-cut, and although water-jet technology is very amenable to mass production, it is not likely that it will successfully compete with inexpensive die-cut cardboard puzzles.

In the pages that follow you will be introduced to the materials, tools, and techniques used to make your own wooden jigsaw puzzles. Chapter 1 looks at tools and materials. Chapter 2 provides instructions for making strip-cut puzzles. Chapter 3 explains how to make puzzles using the fretsaw, a simple hand tool. Chapter 4 introduces free-form puzzles, tray puzzles, layered puzzles, line cutting, and figure pieces. Chapter 5 provides directions for making several puzzles designed to engage the young puzzle enthusiast. Chapter 6 discusses labels, inventories, and boxes. Chapter 7 provides instructions on building shop-made equipment. The book concludes with lists of sources of supplies and references.

One

Getting Started

AT FIRST GLANCE IT MIGHT APPEAR that making a wooden jigsaw puzzle is a simple matter of having a thin piece of wood with a picture on it and a saw with which to cut it into puzzle pieces. But the reality of making a wooden jigsaw puzzle is a bit more complex. You have to select an appropriate picture, prepare the wood, and mount the picture to the wood, then you must select a saw blade, fit it to the saw, and tension it—all before you cut the first puzzle piece.

The Puzzle Picture

The picture chosen for a wooden jigsaw puzzle is a major factor in its success. If the picture is bright and colorful with complex subject matter, then the person putting the puzzle together is going to be invited, by the very nature of the image, to become involved in its assembly. In contrast, if the picture lacks charm and interest and has little color or brilliance, it will not attract the puzzle enthusiast.

A visit to a store selling jigsaw puzzles will reveal what the puzzle manufacturer's believe the public will purchase. Typical subject matter includes copies of works of art, alpine scenes, waterscapes, city street scenes, rural landscapes, and faraway, exotic places. As you gain skill in puzzle making, you also will gain skill in selecting interesting images for puzzles. In fact, you probably will end up with many more pictures than you can possibly cut.

There are some physical factors that also determine a picture's suitability for a jigsaw puzzle. In the process of cutting, the surface of a puzzle is subjected to considerable wear and tear as the puzzle board is turned this way and that to cut the individual pieces. The picture used for the puzzle must be capable of withstanding this wear and still look nice when the puzzle is finished. There are three factors to consider. The first is the weight of the paper. It should feel substantial to the touch—more like an index card than a newspaper. Generally, in printing, heavier weight papers are used when a high-quality color reproduction is desired. The second factor to consider is the quality of the paper. Many papers used for printing pictures are coated with a very thin layer of white clay. Sometimes this can be detected by examining the nonprinted portions of the picture, such as the borders. The clay coating enhances the colors in the picture, giving them a richness and depth that would not otherwise be possible. The surface will be smooth and have a sheen rather than being dull like a sheet of typing paper. The third factor is the quality of the picture itself. Quality color reproductions usually are coated with clear varnish to protect the image. If the surface of the picture has an overall shine, it probably has been coated with varnish. Pictures on heavy-weight, clay-coated paper to which a protective varnish coating has been applied to the colored image work best as puzzles. As with most rules, however, common sense is the best judge. There are some perfectly fine reproductions that are not printed on coated paper and that do not have a varnished surface. Avoid using a picture that feels flimsy, however; it probably will not stand up under the puzzle-making process.

There are numerous sources of images for puzzles. Among the most common are calendars. Many calendars printed today have color reproductions of excellent quality, and the range of images is almost limitless. Once your friends discover that you use calendar pictures for your puzzles, you probably will be deluged with used calendars, especially in January!

Photographs, postcards, and greeting cards also are good sources, but these pictures are usually small. Photographs can be enlarged to almost any size, but the enlargements may present problems when cutting the puzzle. The materials used in making an enlargement will dull saw blades rapidly and slow down the cutting process substantially. An alternative to color enlargements is color photocopying, but this too has its drawbacks, since the paper used is lightweight and there is no protective layer of varnish on the surface of the reproduction. Unless you protect the surface, it will wear rapidly when being cut. (Means of protecting the surface of such pictures are discussed in the next chapter.) Color photocopies can be used for jigsaw puzzle pictures; you just need to be aware of some problems you may encounter. As a matter of fact, most of the puzzles illustrated in this book were made from color photocopies.

Museum shops are one of the best

sources of pictures. Here you will find prints and posters in all sizes and with all kinds of subjects. The pictures themselves are of the highest quality and reasonably priced.

Coffee-table books—that is, books with large color prints—can be inexpensive sources of pictures, especially if you buy the book used or on sale. And even if the initial cost of the book is high, often there are so many pictures in the book that the cost of the individual images will be quite modest.

The selection of a picture for a jigsaw puzzle ultimately is a matter of aesthetics and personal taste. The more exciting the picture in terms of both subject matter and design, the more interesting the finished puzzle will be for the puzzle enthusiast. Here there are no rules and the Latin expression *de gustibus non est disputandum* is the final arbiter: about matters of taste there can be no dispute. Make puzzles from pictures you like, and you will discover others who like the same kinds of puzzles.

An important legal note: *Although there are many pictures available for puzzles, most of them are copyrighted. This means they may not be reproduced or used for commercial purposes without the permission of the copyright owner. Therefore, if you intend to sell any of the puzzles you make, you must be careful to select only those pictures that are in the public domain (that is, pictures whose copyrights have expired) or obtain specific written permission to use the picture.*

The Puzzle Board

The earliest wooden jigsaw puzzles were made from thin panels of mahogany or similar hardwoods, to which the pictures were glued. Because of the relative ease with which a thin piece of wood can split along the grain, the pieces in these early puzzles were cut rather large with no small projections. To overcome this inherent weakness of wood, later puzzles were cut from plywood made of laminations of thin wood veneers with the grain in alternate layers running at right angles to one another. Today, practically all wooden jigsaw puzzles are made from hardwood plywood.

Plywood is not without its limitations, however. There can be voids in the interior layers of veneer where, for example, knots in the sheet of veneer fell out before being glued to the other layers. Such voids may severely weaken the puzzle pieces or, at the very least, present a less-than-perfect appearance. Delamination is another defect of plywood. Delamination occurs when the glue fails to completely bond the layers of veneer together, whether because insufficient glue was used or inadequate heat and pressure were applied during the process of gluing up the sheet of plywood. Delaminated areas in a wooden jigsaw puzzle may result in weak puzzle pieces or even the loss of part of a puzzle piece during the sawing process. Because of the likelihood of encountering such defects, the common fir plywood found in most lumberyards is not suitable for making wooden jigsaw puzzles. In addition, fir plywood tends to tear out easily on the back edges when sawn, rendering the pieces unsightly and difficult to assemble.

Several kinds of plywood suitable for making wooden jigsaw puzzles are commercially available. They are Baltic birch plywood; model aircraft plywood; basswood plywood; and Select Birch, G2S (good two sides) plywood. In the chapters that follow, when a puzzle calls for the use of plywood, any of the four may be used.

Baltic birch plywood in 1/4-inch thickness has five layers, all made from solid birch laminations. It is available from numerous sources in sizes ranging from 1 foot square to 4-by-8-foot sheets. Model aircraft plywood is similar to Baltic birch but may be made from other hardwoods, such as mahogany or maple. It is available at many model or hobby stores in a variety of sizes from 6 inches square up to 1 by 3 feet. Basswood is a softwood, and when made into plywood, it cuts very easily with a scroll saw. It will have considerably more tear-out than hardwood plywoods, however; that is, splintery edges will occur on the back of the plywood as a result of the saw tearing fibers loose from the surface of the wood.

Select Birch, G2S plywood is quite different from the others described above in that a 1/4-inch sheet has only three layers: two thin outer layers and one thick core layer. This plywood is used for paneling and furniture construction where both sides have to present a finished, defect-free appearance. Because the outer layers of this plywood are quite thin, the inner core also has to be defect free. Any voids in the core would telegraph, or show through to the outer surface, and appear as blemishes when the wood is finished. You can be fairly confident that this plywood does not contain voids. Of the four plywoods described, this one is the least expensive and, as it is handled by many industrial plywood companies, the most readily available.

Hardboard (Masonite) can also be used for jigsaw puzzles. Whether or not such a puzzle can be called a wooden jigsaw puzzle is a matter of semantics, since hardboard is made from finely ground wood pulp mixed with glue and pressed into sheets and, thus, has the same basic ingredients as plywood. Hardboard is manufactured in two forms: tempered and untempered. Tempered hardboard is much stiffer and has a harder surface finish than untempered hardboard and is preferred for puzzle making. Hardboard comes in 4-by-8-foot sheets and is sold by most lumberyards. Although hardboard does not have many of the defects of plywood, there are three drawbacks to its use in making puzzles. First, the material is much more difficult to saw than plywood, and therefore it will take more saw blades and more time to cut the puzzle. Second, the fine dust that results from cutting hardboard may be irritating to the nose (although this annoyance may also be experienced by some when cutting plywood). And finally, the cut edges of hardboard are not nearly as interesting as that of plywood. Nevertheless, it will serve for a puzzle board and may even be the best material for painted children's jigsaw puzzles, since it can stand up under a lot of abuse.

Adhesives

The ideal adhesive for gluing the picture to the puzzle board is one that is inexpensive, easy to apply, foolproof to use, and has positive bonding qualities. Also, since wooden jigsaw puzzles tend to be collector's items, the glue needs to be able to withstand a variety of storage conditions. Until recently, casein glue and hide glue were used for this purpose. Casein glue evidently has been supplanted by more modern glues, as it is no longer found in any major woodworking supply catalogs. Hide glue is inexpensive, easy to use, readily available, and ages well. There are two drawbacks to its use, however, that make other adhesives more desirable. When cutting a puzzle made with hide glue, the scroll saw blades dull more quickly than when using other adhesives, and the heat generated causes the glue to burn and give off an unpleasant odor.

Aliphatic resin glues, or yellow glues, have pretty well replaced hide glue in puzzle making. Franklin's Titebond, available through most hardware stores and lumberyards, is one such glue. It is inexpensive, can be brushed or rolled onto the puzzle board easily, and adheres very well. Like most liquid glues, it requires that the puzzle board and picture be clamped between two smooth flat surfaces while the glue sets. Cleanup requires only soap and water. The major disadvantage of using liquid glues such as Titebond over some other adhesives on the market—for example, spray adhesives—is that they require more tools and equipment (clamps, cauls, glue trays, brushes, and rollers) than other adhesives. In addition, the glue must be given time to dry thoroughly (at least twenty-four hours) before the puzzle can be cut. Nevertheless, for making basic wooden jigsaw puzzles, the use of Titebond glue is recommended.

Numerous spray adhesives are available that will give satisfactory results in adhering pictures to puzzle boards and also have many other uses in puzzle making. Spray adhesives may present health hazards in the form of the solvents and propellants, and you need to have adequate ventilation when using these materials. Another disadvantage to spray adhesives is that they sometimes form a gummy mixture with the sawdust when the puzzle is being cut. This residue can be difficult to remove if it adheres to the surface of the puzzle pieces. Nevertheless, these adhesives can be indispensable in making certain kinds of jigsaw puzzles. Use 3M's

Super 77 or a similar adhesive whenever a spray adhesive is required.

Another type of spray adhesive that is useful for a number of puzzle-making processes is a repositionable one, such as 3M's ReMount Repositionable Adhesive. This adhesive will hold a piece of paper securely to a surface yet allow the paper to be removed and adhered to another surface without losing its tack and without leaving any residue behind. Use it or a similar adhesive whenever a repositionable spray adhesive is recommended.

There also are thermo-setting adhesives, which melt and bond with other surfaces when pressure and heat are applied. Probably the most commonly known is dry mount tissue, used to adhere photographs or prints to display boards and other surfaces. It can also be used to adhere a picture to a puzzle board and will produce a blemish-free surface. It comes in sheet form and requires the use of a dry-mount press to join the two surfaces together. Dry mount presses are expensive, however, especially in the larger sizes needed for jigsaw puzzles. *Do not use dry mount tissue or any other thermo-setting adhesive on color photocopies;* the color pigment of the photocopy is fused onto the surface of the paper with heat and pressure in a process similar to that used for these adhesives, and the color may lift off the print and transfer onto the cover paper.

Other adhesives, including rubber cement, model airplane glue, and low-tack drafting (*not* masking) tape will be needed for a number of tasks in puzzle making. These will be specified when their use is necessary for a particular puzzle.

Abrasive Papers

You will need to use abrasive paper to sand away loose wood fibers both when cutting the plywood puzzle boards to size and after cutting the puzzle itself. Abrasive papers are available in a variety of grits and abrasive materials. I prefer garnet paper over silicon carbide paper, but both have good cutting qualities. Five different grits, #100, #150, #220, #280, and #600, will cover the variety of sanding tasks you encounter in this book. The grit you will use most is #150. Whenever abrasive paper is called for, use this grit size unless some other grit is specified. A padded sanding block and a sanding board are useful for many of the sanding tasks. (Instructions for making them are found in chapter 7.)

Wood Filler

In making puzzle boards for wooden jigsaw puzzles, you occasionally will find a defect, such as a crack, chip, or dent, in the surface of the plywood. If not repaired, this might detract from the appearance of the puzzle. In many instances, such defects can be repaired with wood filler. Wood filler is made from a combination of finely ground wood fibers, called wood flour, and a binding material such as glue. One such wood filler is Durham's Rock Hard Wood Putty. *Note:* Do not confuse this wood filler with the wood filler used to fill the pores in wood prior to applying a finish.

Wood Finishes

A wood finish may be used to protect the back of the puzzle board, to emphasize the grain of the wood, and to bind the surface fibers of the wood together helping to minimize tear-out when cutting. There is a disadvantage to using a finish, however, in that it makes the puzzle more difficult to cut, increasing both the time and the number of saw blades required.

The most appropriate finish for the back of the puzzle board is either a phenolic resin finish such as Watco's Danish Oil Finish or a tung oil like Miniwax's Tung Oil. Oil finishes have two advantages. They are easy to apply—just brush them on or wipe them on with a soft, clean cloth. And they can be refreshed after the puzzle back has been sanded following cutting. Use a cloth just dampened with the oil finish so that none will run through the spaces in the puzzle and get onto the picture. Cleanup, if you use a brush to apply the oil, requires a brush cleaner or paint thinner followed by soap and water. Properly dispose of any cloths or paper towels used with the oil because of the possibility of spontaneous combustion. First wash the cloths with soap and water and spread them out to dry, then store them and any paper towels in an air-tight container.

Some puzzles, such as the map puzzle and the Noah's Ark puzzle in chapter 5, are painted. A nontoxic, water-based acrylic paint is satisfactory for this purpose. It is readily available from art stores and craft shops. Use a wood sealer to provide a foundation for the paint. Numerous wood sealers are available at paint and hardware stores. Some of them raise the grain of the wood; test the sealer on a scrap of wood before applying it to the puzzle pieces. Whichever sealer you choose, be sure to follow the manufacturer's instructions.

Saws for Puzzles

There are three saws associated with the cutting of wooden jigsaw puzzles: the fretsaw, jigsaw, and scroll saw. The fretsaw is a hand-powered tool, whereas the other two saws are powered by some other source of energy. The fretsaw has a C-shaped frame with a handle fastened to the lower leg of the frame. Clamps with thumbscrews are mounted at the end of each leg of the frame to hold the saw blade. The throat of the fretsaw, the distance from the saw blade to the back of the frame, varies from 8 to 24 inches. The deeper the throat, the larger the puzzle it can cut. Fretsaws are designed to use standard 5-inch scroll saw and jeweler's saw blades. The saw blades are tensioned by springing the two ends of the saw frame toward one another while clamping the blade in place.

Although they are still called jigsaw

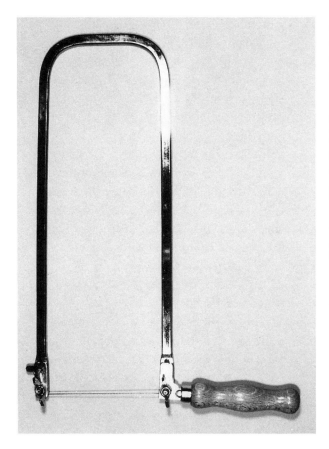

Before the advent of jigsaws and scroll saws, puzzles were cut with fretsaws. Fretsaws use the same blades as scroll saws and jigsaws.

again. This up and down motion, known as jigging, is intended to attract fish to the bait. It is believed that the jigsaw got its name from this fishing technique, because the up and down motion of its blade resembles the motion of the fishing line when jigging.

The scroll saw, in contrast, got its name because of its ability to cut a wide variety of curved lines and other intricate shapes. Much nineteenth- and early-twentieth-century architecture had complex wooden ornamentation. For example, a Greek Revival house might have wooden Ionic columns with scrolled capitals, and it is from cutting such architectural ornaments that the scroll saw received its name.

puzzles, today most wooden puzzles are likely cut on scroll saws. The name jigsaw puzzle is used to describe any puzzle with intricate straight and curved shapes such a machine can cut, but it can be made with a jigsaw, scroll saw, or with a fretsaw. Let's look at the differences between the jigsaw and the scroll saw.

There is a technique in fishing that involves dropping a baited hook and line into the water and, once the bait reaches the desired depth, jerking it upward a short distance and then dropping it

The two saws usually differ in terms of the mechanical action of the saw blade. In the jigsaw, the entire mechanism is held in a rigid, C-shaped frame. The blade is held at its lower end in a clamp fastened to a vertical rod that moves up and down in a straight line. The upper end of the blade is held in a second clamp fastened to a spring attached to the upper arm of the saw's frame. The spring serves to maintain the saw blade under tension at all times. Because of the way it is held, the path of the jigsaw blade is perpendicular to the saw table.

In the scroll saw, the lower end of the saw blade is held in a clamp at the end of an arm that pivots on a bearing toward the rear of the saw frame. The upper end of the saw blade is held in a clamp at the end of a second arm that also pivots on a bearing toward the rear of the saw frame. Extensions of both arms toward the rear of the machines are connected to one another with a spring that provides tension on the saw blade. The two arms, the spring connecting them, and the saw blade form a parallelogram with a rocking

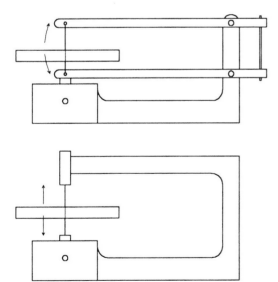

A scroll saw blade (top) cuts a shallow arc through the wood it is cutting, whereas a jigsaw blade (bottom) cuts straight up and down. There is no discernible difference in the action of the two saws when cutting jigsaw puzzles.

motion around the bearings. The path of the scroll saw appears to be perpendicular to the saw table but, in fact, describes a shallow arc. Thus, the jigsaw and scroll saw can be differentiated according to the path the saw blade follows. For convenience in the following discussion, the term scroll saw will also apply to the jigsaw.

If you are planning to buy a scroll saw, some features to consider are depth of throat, speed controls, and blade clamps. The depth of throat determines the maximum size puzzle the saw can cut. As with the fretsaw, the depth of throat is measured from the back edge of the saw blade to the front edge of the rear frame member. Scroll saws are manufactured with a variety of throat depths ranging from 12 to 24 or more inches. All other things being equal, you should buy the scroll saw with the deepest throat, as this will increase the range of sizes of wooden jigsaw puzzles you can cut.

The relationship between the depth of throat and puzzle size is straightforward in that when cutting an interlock (the knob and socket that hold the puzzle pieces together), it is necessary to rotate the puzzle board almost 360 degrees. Keep an eye on the travel of one corner of a puzzle board when you're cutting a puzzle and you'll find that it does indeed make an almost complete circle around the saw blade.

Now imagine an interlock being at the midpoint of the long side of a puzzle board. The distance measured from this point to the farthest corner on the opposite side is the minimum depth of throat needed to cut the puzzle. Add 1/2 inch or so to the measured length to provide a margin for error. As a consequence, a scroll saw with an 18-inch throat can cut a puzzle slightly less than 16 inches square and, of course, longer and narrower puzzles to the degree that the distance measured from the midpoint of the long side to the farthest corner is somewhat less than 18 inches.

The size of noninterlocking puzzles (chapter 4) that can be cut on a scroll saw can be almost twice that of an interlocking puzzle, because the puzzle board need not be rotated while cutting. Cuts can be made from each side of the puzzle and joined at the midpoint.

Different materials require different speeds for cutting. Materials like metal, bone, and plastic need to be cut at very low speeds, whereas plywood, hardwood, and softwood can be cut at increasingly higher speeds. As a rule of thumb, the harder and thicker the material, the lower the cutting speed, and the softer or thinner the material, the higher the cutting speed. Also, cutting intricate pieces requires lower speeds than simple ones. Cutting speeds are usually given in terms of the number of up and down strokes the blade makes per minute (SPM). Some saws run at a single speed, ranging from 800 to 1,720 SPM. The Delta 13-inch scroll saw, for example, runs at 1,700 SPM. Some saws use steppulleys to pro-

vide two, three, or four different speeds. A typical two-speed saw, Reliant Model AL18, has a low speed of 850 SPM and a high speed of 1,720 SPM. Changing speeds on a machine with step pulleys is achieved by shifting the drive belt from one set of pulleys to another, either manually or through the use of a lever. Other scroll saws are equipped with variable-speed motors that enable you to change speeds simply by turning a knob. The Delta 20-inch variable-speed saw and the Hegner Multimax variable-speed scroll saws allow you to select any speed between 400 and 1,800 SPM.

For making wooden jigsaw puzzles, a scroll saw with a variable-speed motor is best. It enables you to select the most comfortable cutting speed for the task at hand. For example, when cutting strip-cut puzzles, a speed of 1,200 SPM might work well, whereas in cutting an intricate figure piece, you might want to slow the speed to 500 SPM. Also, should you break a blade in the middle of a cut, setting the saw at its lowest speed might enable you to retrace the path of the saw blade with a new blade without removing an appreciable amount of wood.

Blade clamps are devices used to connect the saw blade to the upper and lower arms of the scroll saw. They may employ thumbscrews, hex bolts, or separate clamping blocks, depending on the design of the saw. With some scroll saws, replacing a blade can be a very challenging experience. In cutting a wooden jigsaw puzzle, you may find it necessary to replace the blade a half dozen or more times, so it is imperative that this feature of the scroll saw be both easy to use and dependable in gripping the saw blade. Clamping blocks are probably the easiest blade-clamping device to use. The blade's ends are fastened in the clamping blocks outside the saw and then, as an assembly, snapped into holders on the scroll saw. If possible, try changing a blade several times on a scroll saw you're thinking of purchasing.

Scroll saws may be used to cut a wide variety of materials: wood, bone, plastic, metal, even ceramics and glass. Different kinds of saw blades are needed to cut these materials, and even with a given material such as wood, one blade size may be used for thick wood and another for thin wood. Knowing about some of the different types of blades will help you decide which blade to use for cutting a specific jigsaw puzzle.

The standard scroll saw blade is 5 inches in length and has plain ends. Some scroll saws on the market, however, use pin-end blades or blades that are longer or shorter than the standard blade. A saw that uses standard blades offers the greatest choice of blade sizes and styles, whereas with a saw that uses nonstandard blades, there are fewer options and limited sources from which to obtain such blades.

Scroll saw blades are identified by the blade size (#2/0, #1/0, #1, or #2), by the number of teeth per inch (12, 15, 32, or 48), and by the style of the blade (standard, skip-tooth, double-skip-tooth, and reversed-tooth). The blade size indicates its width and thickness. The width of the blade determines both its overall strength and the radius of a curve it can follow. Although a wide blade may be stronger, a narrower blade can cut a smaller radius. The thickness of the blade coupled with the set of the teeth determines the kerf, or width of the cut. The set is the distance the teeth of the saw are offset from the centerline of the blade. Set is used to provide clearance for the saw blade so that it does not bind in the cut. The kerf refers to how much wood the blade removes when cutting and, in terms of wooden jigsaw puzzles, determines how tightly the pieces fit back together. In general, a puzzle that has tight-fitting pieces is preferable to one with a loose fit. In fact, some puzzle cutters and puzzle enthusiasts believe that you should be able to pick up a puzzle by one of its corners and it should remain intact. As will be discussed later, however, there are times when loose-fitting pieces are actually preferable.

The number of teeth per inch (TPI) of a scroll saw blade relates directly to the smoothness of the cut. The fewer teeth, the coarser the cut; the more teeth, the finer the cut. Regardless of the number of teeth, there always will be some tearout on the back side of the wood being cut, caused by the teeth tearing some of the fibers free from the wood rather than cutting them. Many efforts have been made in blade design to eliminate tear-out, resulting in such improvements as the skip-tooth, double-skip-tooth, and reversed-tooth blades. The skip-tooth blade has a space between every other tooth. This space provides a place for sawdust to accumulate during cutting, thereby reducing friction, heat, and binding, which in turn reduces the amount of tear-out. The double-skip-tooth blade serves the same purpose and has two teeth removed at each gap, with either a single tooth or double tooth between spaces. In the reversed-tooth blade design, the last four to six teeth point upward rather than in the normal downward direction. These teeth cut when the saw blade is moving upward, thereby eliminating tear-out on the bottom of the wood being sawn. Unfortunately, with thin woods such as the plywood used for jigsaw puzzles, the teeth of the reversed-tooth blade exit at the top surface of the puzzle, thus producing tear-out on the surface of the picture. Additionally, the reversed-tooth design tends to lift the wood from the saw table, making cutting more difficult and prone to error. For these reasons, reversed-tooth scroll saw blades are not used for cutting wooden jigsaw puzzles, although they may be found useful in other aspects of puzzle making.

Though you might assume that a 2/0 saw blade by one manufacturer is the same width and thickness and has the

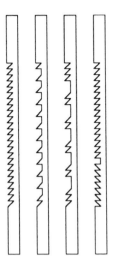

Four types of scroll saw blades are used in cutting jigsaw puzzles. They are, from left to right, standard, skip-tooth, double-skip-tooth, and reversed-tooth. The skip-tooth and double-skip-tooth produce the least tear-out on the back of the puzzle board. When cutting puzzles from thicker wood, the reversed-tooth blade also may be used to reduce tear-out.

same number of teeth as one made by another manufacturer, this is not the case. For example, Advanced Machinery Import's 2/0 blade (AP2/0) has thirty-seven teeth per inch and is .024 inches wide and .011 inches thick, whereas Wildwood Design's 2/0 Eberle blade (4000ST) has thirty-three teeth per inch, and is .024 inches wide and .009 inches thick, and Constantine's 2/0 blade (0B440) has twenty-eight teeth per inch and is .022 inches wide and .010 inches thick. The differences are significant. They have a direct impact on not only how the blades cut, but also how the saw cuts appear. Subtle differences among scroll saw blades also may be encountered. For example, Eberle saw blades are treated with a copper-colored coating, presumably to dissipate the heat generated during cutting.

The only way to determine which blades work best for you is through experimentation. Buy a dozen or more of several different kinds of saw blades, and try them out while cutting similar puzzles under similar circumstances. The one that works best is the one you should use.

Some companies sell assortments of scroll saw blades that are useful for getting acquainted with a particular scroll saw and its capabilities. Usually, however, scroll saw blades of a specific size and type are sold only by the dozen or the gross. Scroll saw blades are packaged in at least three different ways: in plastic envelopes, wrapped with a relatively large-diameter copper wire, and wrapped with a very fine iron wire. The plastic envelope is easily opened and the coarse wire wrapping is easily removed. The fine wire wrapping found on many packages of scroll saw blades can be quite difficult to remove, however. The simplest way to deal with this wrapping is to insert the pointed end of a hobby knife blade, with its edge pointing upward and away from you, under the tight coils at one end of the wrapping. Now push through the coils, thereby cutting them. Repeat for the coils at the opposite end. The remaining wire then can be removed easily.

Tools for Trimming Pictures

You'll need a straightedge for trimming the puzzle picture. A 12-inch, 30-by-60 degree clear acrylic triangle serves well for this purpose, because it enables you to see the picture beneath it as you are trimming the border. Any ruler with a metal edge can also be used as a straightedge. A 12-by-18-inch self-healing cutting mat, available at art stores, provides a good surface on which to cut the picture. This mat is relatively unabrasive and will not dull your knife blades as quickly as other surfaces. Lacking such a mat, you can use hardboard or thick cardboard to protect the workbench while trimming. Use a hobby knife such as an X-acto for trimming the puzzle picture. It should have a sharp, pointed blade so that the paper will be cut rather than torn. A small hone for sharpening the knife blade is also useful. You'll also need a ruler and pencil for measuring and marking out puzzle boards.

Equipment for Gluing Pictures

Although you can use a brush to apply the glue to the puzzle board and weights such as bricks to hold the puzzle board and picture down against a flat surface while the glue sets, much more dependable and professional results are obtained by using more specialized equipment. You'll need a glue tray, a support block for the glue tray, a small paint roller, a stop block for the puzzle board, cauls, and C-clamps.

For the glue tray, use a shallow plastic tray about 6 inches wide, 15 inches long, and 2 inches deep. You can find such a tray in the housewares section of most department stores. In addition, you'll need a piece of scrap wood 3/4 inch thick, an inch or so wide, and the width of the tray in length to raise one end of the glue tray so that the glue will remain in the opposite end. If you intend to glue up a number of puzzle boards over a short period of time, you'll also need a cover for the glue tray to prevent the moisture in the glue from evaporating. A thin piece of acrylic plastic or plywood can be used. If you use plywood, you need to apply a finish such as polyurethane varnish to it to prevent moisture from the glue from being absorbed into the plywood cover, thereby causing it to warp. A 3-inch paint roller with a cover of fine foam should be used to apply the glue to the surface of the plywood. The roller cover should be removable for cleaning.

A stop block made of a piece of 1/8-inch hardboard or thin wood approximately 3 inches wide and 8 inches long is clamped to the end of the workbench. The plywood puzzle board is butted up against this stop block to keep it from shifting position when you apply the glue.

You'll also need two cauls (see chapter 7), smooth, flat boards used for pressing the picture against the surface of the puzzle board, along with six or more 3-inch C-clamps, depending on the size of the puzzle being glued.

Quilter's Thimble

If you spend much time cutting wooden jigsaw puzzles, you may find one or more of your fingers, especially on the left hand, becoming sore from pressing down on the sharp edges of the puzzle pieces while cutting the puzzle board. If you continue sawing over a long period of time, calluses will develop on these fingers. You can protect your fingers with a device known as a quilter's thimble. It is made of leather and is held in place on the finger with an elastic band. (A quilter's thimble is shown on the scroll saw table in chapter 7.) Quilter's thimbles are available at most stores that sell quilting supplies.

Other tools and materials that are useful for puzzle making will be discussed as necessary in later chapters. For now, let's get on to the actual process of making a wooden jigsaw puzzle.

Two

Basic Puzzle-Making Techniques

THE FIRST PUZZLE-MAKING TECH-nique you need to learn is how to make strip-cut puzzles with interlocking pieces. Strip cutting is an excellent process for the beginning puzzle cutter; it teaches you to be precise in cutting so that each piece securely interlocks with all adjoining pieces. Strip cutting involves first cutting the puzzle into a series of strips with interlocking edges, and then cutting the strips into individual interlocking pieces. Since interlocking pieces are at the heart of most wooden jigsaw puzzles, you need to understand how they work.

The most common puzzle interlock design consists of a knob that extends outward from one puzzle piece and fits into a socket cut into the adjacent puzzle piece. Both the knob and the socket are cut simultaneously and will fit exactly into one another. As can be noted in the drawing, the knob narrows where it joins the body of the puzzle piece. This narrowing of the knob locks it into its socket. In a simple strip-cut puzzle, each piece (except for the edge and corner pieces) has either a knob or a socket on each side. As a result, there are six basic shapes a strip-cut piece may have. Edge and corner pieces are simply variants of these six shapes, having no knobs or sockets on their outer edges. More complex strip-cut puzzles may have multiple interlocks on several sides.

In order to interlock, the head of the knob should be at least twice the thickness of the saw kerf wider than the neck of the knob. Any narrower than this and the piece can be pulled out of its socket. The narrower the neck of the knob,

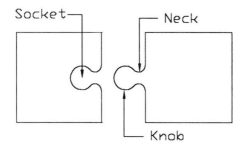

The interlock serves to hold the puzzle pieces together. It consists of a knob, socket, and neck. If the neck of the interlock is too wide relative to the width of the knob, the interlock will not hold.

within practicality, the more positive the interlocking function. The knob and socket can be any shape desired as long as the neck is appropriately narrow. Some variations on the simple knob and socket design are shown in the accompanying illustration. In practice, a smooth, flowing curve works best—and looks best, too.

Practice Puzzles

Cutting some practice puzzles will help you better understand the principle of the interlock and will teach you some basic puzzle-cutting techniques. Begin by cutting a 4-by-8-foot sheet of 1/4-inch plywood into 4-by-4-foot or smaller sections before cutting the puzzle boards to size. The smaller panels are much easier to handle. It is very difficult to accurately cut a long, straight line with a scroll saw; a table saw is much better suited to cutting the plywood down to size. Use a blade with carbide teeth specifically designed for cutting plywood in order to produce the cleanest cut.

Now cut six 3-by-3-inch squares from the plywood. If you wish, you can also practice adhering pictures to the puzzle boards, although it is not necessary at this point. Take some color illustrations or advertisements from an old magazine,

The shapes of strip-cut puzzle pieces vary according to the placement of knobs and sockets and according to whether they are inner, edge, or corner pieces.

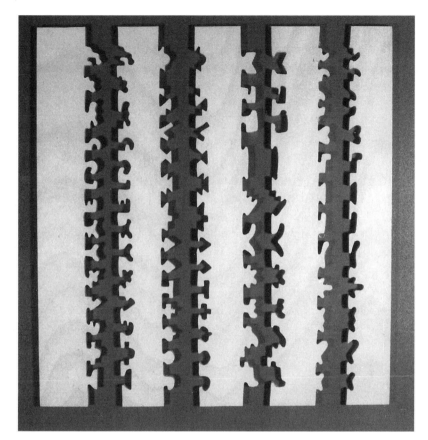

These sample interlocks demonstrate the wide range of shapes they may take. Varying the shape of the interlocks can add visual interest to a jigsaw puzzle.

and cut six 3¹/4-by-3¹/4-inch squares from them so that you have a picture for each square of plywood. Also cut two 3¹/2-by-3¹/2-inch squares of ³/4-inch plywood or lumber with a smooth surface. Sand off any rough edges or splinters with abrasive paper. These will serve as cauls to apply pressure when you glue the pictures to the plywood squares.

Lay one of your puzzle pictures face down on a clean piece of paper. Brush and wipe off any sawdust from one of the plywood squares. Pour a small amount of glue in a shallow dish or lid and, using a small brush with stiff bristles, apply a thin, even coat of glue to one side of the plywood square, brushing it on in the direction of the grain. Rotate the square 90 degrees and apply another thin coat of glue to the plywood, this time brushing it on across the grain. Turn the square another 90 degrees and even out the two coats of glue with the brush.

Now center the plywood square, glue side down, over the back of the picture so that there is an even border on all sides. Press the plywood firmly against the picture to be sure it is well adhered.

Then turn the picture face up and smooth out any wrinkles. Work carefully and rapidly, because the moisture absorbed from the glue will make the paper tear easily.

Place the glued-up puzzle board face down on one of the clamping cauls, place the second caul on top of the plywood, and put the sandwiched assembly in a C-clamp or vise, or use a heavy weight to apply pressure. Leave the puzzle board clamped for at least twenty minutes, then remove it from the clamping cauls and allow it to set overnight. Glue up the remaining practice squares following the same procedures. Then clean the glue brush with soap and water and discard any leftover glue.

After the glue has dried, use a hobby knife to cut off the portion of the picture's border extending beyond the edges of the plywood. Remove any rough edges remaining with abrasive paper using a sanding block. The piece of plywood with the picture glued to it is known as a *prepared puzzle board*.

With a pencil, draw two perpendicular lines on top of one of the puzzle boards, either plain or prepared, intersecting at the center of the square. This will divide the practice piece into four $1^1/2$-inch squares. Fit the scroll saw with a #1 blade (or a #2/0 blade if you are adventurous and have some skill in using a scroll saw) with the teeth pointing down. Adjust the tension on the blade until it makes a high-pitched, musical sound when plucked with a fingernail. This tension helps to ensure that the blade will cut vertically even if the wood is pushed slightly out of alignment to the right or left. With the saw motor turned off, rub the saw blade gently up and down with your finger to double-check that the teeth are pointing downward toward the saw table and outward, away from the throat of the saw. You should be able to feel the roughness of the teeth as your finger moves upward and much less roughness as your finger moves downward against the blade. Make it a habit to check the direction of the saw teeth in this manner every time you change a blade. If you begin cutting a jigsaw puzzle with an upside-down blade, the edges of the picture will be ragged where cut and almost impossible to repair. If you inadvertently put the blade in backward with the teeth pointing to the rear of the saw, as I have done on occasion, the saw blade simply will not cut.

If the scroll saw has a variable-speed motor or other means to control the speed, set the saw speed to around 1,000 SPM. Experiment with the saw speeds as you cut different puzzles until you find the one best suited to your cutting style. As a rule of thumb, the higher the saw speed, the quicker the puzzle pieces can be cut, but the less control you have over the cutting and the greater the likelihood that errors will be more serious.

Your scroll saw probably has both a hold-down foot and a blade guard designed to protect you and the piece of wood you're cutting. When cutting the small pieces used in wooden jigsaw puzzles, however, you may find that both the guard and the hold-down foot are hindrances when manipulating the puzzle board around all the necessary curves. For this reason, some puzzle cutters remove both devices from their scroll saws. There is very little chance of serious injury when cutting a puzzle without the guard, because the blade is so fine that if you should accidentally come in contact with it, usually only a minor scratch or cut will result. Use your own judgment in this matter, however; only you can determine how much risk you should take.

Study the drawings of the puzzle interlock and the various shapes puzzle pieces may take. When you can form a good mental image of an interlock, turn the saw on and align the blade with one of the pencil lines drawn on the practice square. Begin sawing by pressing the piece of plywood into the moving saw blade. Hold the piece of plywood with both hands, the right hand doing the steering and the left hand holding the plywood down close to the blade. When you are almost halfway to the perpendicular centerline, begin cutting the first interlock. You can cut it to either the right or left of the main line. As you make the turns around the knob, try to maintain a constant forward movement of the piece into the saw blade. You will have to visualize the shape of the inter-

lock, and if you should stray from that mental image, as you probably will, *do not back up!* Backing up and restarting the cut will result in an ugly-looking interlock that will stand out as an obvious error. Instead, slow down and keep cutting forward, making gradual corrections to produce the best-shaped interlock you can. As you complete the cutting of the interlock, mentally prepare yourself for returning to cutting a straight line.

Continue cutting along the path of the main line, past the centerline, and to the point where you think the second interlock should begin. Cut the second interlock in the opposite direction from the first interlock. Again, maintain constant forward pressure when cutting the plywood, and *never* back up in the saw cut. Try to use smooth, flowing curves when leaving the main line, when cutting the interlock, and when returning to the main line. The more fluid the lines, the more graceful the puzzle pieces will appear.

Occasionally the saw blade may bind or catch and pull the puzzle board out of your grip. This occurs especially when working with a small piece of plywood or when only one or two pieces remain to be cut, and the weight of the piece of plywood is not heavy enough to overcome the pull of the saw blade on its upward stroke. This also may occur if you relax the downward pressure of your hands. The natural tendency is to try to grab the bouncing piece of plywood and

Cutting practice puz-
zles allows you to
learn basic puzzle-cut-
ting techniques while
progressing from sim-
ple four-piece puzzles
(left) to more complex
nine- and sixteen-
piece puzzles (right).

press it back down against the saw table. Don't do it—this will usually result in a jagged hole in the puzzle board. Instead, allow the piece of wood to continue to bounce up and down while you switch off the scroll saw's motor. When the blade comes to a stop, press the plywood back down until it rests on the saw table. Then hold it down firmly with one hand while you switch on the saw motor with the other. Once the blade rides freely in the saw cut, you can resume cutting.

When you have finished cutting the first line, your practice square will separate into two interlocking strips, each with a knob and a socket. You now need

to cut each of these strips down its centerline, forming an interlock in the same manner as above. Again, the interlocks can be cut to the right or left of the centerline as desired. When you have completed cutting the two strips, you'll have four puzzle pieces that can be put back together to form a square.

Rub the back of each piece on a sheet of abrasive paper or a sanding board to remove any splinters or loose fibers of wood, then start putting the four pieces back together again. Examine how each piece interlocks with the two other pieces it joins. Try pulling the interlocked pieces sideways. Do they pull apart? If so, your interlock has too wide a neck. Does the knob look as though you could easily snap it off from the body of the piece? If so, the neck is too narrow. Do the projections at the edge of the socket look fragile and apt to break if too much pressure is applied when you put the pieces together? If so, more gentle curves are needed. Are some of the knobs difficult to fit into the sockets? Will they go in from only one direction—from the bottom up or top down? If this is the case, the cut sides of the interlocks probably are not perpendicular. If a knob is wider at the bottom than at the top, it will fit into its socket only from the bottom up; if a socket is narrower at the bottom than at the top, it can be placed on the knob only from the bottom up. There are two probable causes for such poor fits. You may have inadvertently been pressing the piece of plywood to the right or left of the saw blade's normal path when cutting the puzzle pieces, or else the saw table is not perpendicular to the saw blade.

You can check on the first condition by examining the knobs to see if they have a slight slant. If they do, check the sides of the straight cuts to see if they too slant. If the slanting appears in one area of the cut but not another, or if the edges slant sometimes in one direction and then the other, you can be pretty sure that you were pressing the piece of plywood to one side or the other while cutting. If both the knobs and the straight sides slant, check the saw table to see if it

is square to the blade. The easiest way to do this is to press a length of $3/4$-inch or thicker wood into the saw blade when the saw is running, and cut into the wood $1/16$ inch or so. Turn the saw off and rotate the piece of wood 180 degrees on the saw table so that the slot just cut faces toward you but also is behind the blade. Compare the angle of the saw cut with that of the blade. They should be exactly parallel to one another. If not, then the saw table is out of square and needs to be adjusted. Follow the directions in your saw manual to make the needed correction. Once you have made the adjustment, check the cut again as described above. Do not use the pointed arrow on the saw protractor to align the saw, as this arrow will provide only a partial degree of accuracy.

If the saw cuts an accurate perpendicular line, then watch the blade carefully as it exits a cut. If the blade moves to the right or left as it leaves the cut, perhaps making a pinging sound, then you have been forcing the blade out of its vertical alignment. Should this be the case, you will need to change the manner in which you hold down and manipulate the plywood while sawing it. Each individual needs to adopt a method of holding the wood while sawing that is appropriate for him or her. I hold the puzzle board with the middle finger of my left hand quite close in front but slightly to the left of the saw blade. This finger exerts downward pressure on the plywood and takes the place of the machine's hold-down foot. This finger also serves as a pivot when I'm cutting interlocks or other curves. The remaining fingers on my left hand also exert a downward pressure but to a lesser degree. The hold-down pressure exerted by my left hand is just enough to prevent the plywood from bouncing up and down with the saw blade. Every once in a while I release this downward pressure so that the blade can recenter itself if I've pressed it to the right or left of the cutting line. I hold the outer edge of the puzzle board with my right hand, turning the plywood as necessary to follow the straight lines and curves of the puzzle pieces.

Frequently, especially while you're learning to cut a puzzle, the scroll saw blade will break in the middle of a cut, sometimes for no apparent reason. This can be very disconcerting when you are halfway around the cutting of an interlock. There are three major reasons for blade breakage: the blade has become dull, it has been improperly clamped in the scroll saw, or the blade has been severely twisted or distorted while cutting. And sometimes a blade will break for no reason at all—even when it is not cutting anything. This leads to the notion that a scroll saw blade may break simply by being looked at!

The most usual cause of blade breakage, however, is a worn, dull blade. If the blade breaks in the middle of its length, it is usually because the blade has become

dull and has overheated because of the increasing pressure needed to force it to cut. Sometimes a blade will become dull after just a few minutes of cutting. Other times you may be able to cut an entire puzzle without the blade dulling. This disparity may be due to variations in the manufacturing of the blades or differences in the kinds of wood being cut. Whatever the cause, blade breakage is one of the givens in puzzle cutting. The average number of blades needed to cut a relatively small puzzle is about a half dozen.

There are several clues to when a blade has become worn and needs to be changed. First, it requires increased forward pressure on the plywood being sawn to force the blade to cut. Evidence of such excessive use of feed pressure is a loud pinging sound made by the blade as it exits a cut without snapping either to the right or left of its normal path. Second, the blade will seem to have a mind of its own and will cut increasingly smaller knobs on interlocks and similar curves. Third, you will smell the odor of burning wood. Since it is always better to replace a blade before it breaks, whenever any of these clues become apparent, stop cutting at the first appropriate opportunity and fit a new blade to the saw.

Blade breakage because of improper clamping occurs when the clamp is overtightened, causing the metal to be deformed and weakened where it exits the clamp. Suspect blade breakage from overtightening any time a very small portion of the blade is found in the clamp. Blade breakage because of clamping also may occur if the blade is not vertical to the saw table but leaves the clamp at an angle other than perpendicular. Such improper clamping distorts or twists the blade in a front-to-back direction and may be suspected if a short portion of the blade protrudes from the clamp.

Sometimes when a blade breaks, especially in the middle or at the upper clamp, a portion of the blade may remain embedded in the plywood. Look carefully where the saw cut ended when the blade broke, and remove any broken pieces of saw blade with a pair of long-nosed pliers.

If your scroll saw uses blade clamps that are not an integral part of the saw—that is, one in which the blades are first fitted to the clamps, and then the clamped blade assembly inserted into clamp holders in the saw—it might be worthwhile to purchase several pairs of clamps. This will enable you to have more than one blade prepared ahead of time so that you can quickly replace a blade when it breaks. Moreover, when all the blades in all the clamps are dull or broken, this would be a good time to take a break from cutting while replacing the blades in the clamps.

Probably the worst possible time for a blade to break is when you are halfway around an interlock and halfway along the strip being cut. Faced with this situation, after inserting a new blade into the saw clamps and tightening it to the proper tension, what should you do? If your scroll saw has a variable-speed motor, once you have set it at its lowest speed, it may be possible to reenter the saw cut and follow it to its end without removing an appreciable amount of wood from the saw kerf. When you reach the end of the cut, increase the motor speed and continue cutting.

Another solution, and the only practical one if your saw does not have a variable-speed motor, is to start a new saw cut, either at the opposite end of the puzzle board where the original saw cut would exit, or perpendicular to the line being sawn just below the partially sawn interlock. On a practice square, starting at the opposite end of the cut being made would be the simplest. When cutting large jigsaw puzzles, however, it is often preferable to cut across the strip and then upward to intersect the cut at the point where the blade broke. If you are cutting a puzzle board and decide to begin a new cut from the opposite end, you will need to determine before beginning the cut whether the first interlock cut should be to the right or left of the centerline in relation to the last interlock you cut. Similarly, if you decide to make a crosscut to join the line being cut, you need to determine on which side of the line to make the interlock. Additionally, on this cut you have to anticipate where the crosscut line will intersect with the line you were cutting when the blade broke, make a right-angle turn there, and continue the cut up and around the interlock until you meet the end of the other saw cut. Whichever method you use, do not attempt to separate the sawn piece from the practice square or puzzle board while the saw is running; to do so probably would result in damage to the piece. Instead, turn the saw motor off, and when the blade stops, lift the piece free from the uncut portion of the plywood.

Once you have analyzed the cutting of your first practice square, select a second one and draw perpendicular lines on it in the same manner. Keeping in mind the errors that occurred when you cut the first square, cut the second square into four puzzle pieces. After cutting all four pieces, fit them together and check for cutting errors as before. Continue cutting practice squares this way until you feel you are beginning to acquire some skill in cutting the interlocking pieces.

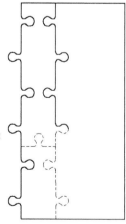

Breaking a blade is a common occurrence when cutting jigsaw puzzles. This diagram shows two different paths that may be followed to reach the point where the blade broke.

Now select another practice square, and this time cut the four interlocking pieces without drawing any guidelines. When cutting an actual puzzle, you will be unable to draw guidelines because portions of them would remain visible on the picture after the puzzle was cut, detracting from its appearance.

Continue to evaluate your puzzle pieces after each cutting exercise. When you feel you are ready to move on to a more complex level, take another practice square and this time divide it with pencil lines into three vertical 1-inch strips and three 1-inch cross strips. Following these lines, first cut the practice puzzle into three interlocking vertical strips, and then cut each of these strips into three interlocking pieces, or nine pieces in all. In this exercise, you have to reduce the size of the interlocks in order to keep them in scale with the smaller-sized puzzle pieces. To achieve this, you will have to describe smaller curves when turning the practice square while cutting the interlocks.

Once you have successfully cut the nine-piece practice square, you're ready to cut the final, sixteen-piece practice square. This practice square will need to be cut into four interlocking vertical strips, and each of these strips into four interlocking pieces. Instead of drawing lines across the surface, this time make vertical marks 3/4 inch apart on two opposite edges of the practice square. Use these marks as starting and ending points for cutting the practice square into strips. Then cut each strip into four interlocking pieces.

The first practice puzzles had pieces about $1^1/2$ inches square. This would be an appropriate size for puzzle pieces for a very young child, from three to six years of age. The second set of practice puzzles had pieces about 1 inch square, appropriate for children from six to ten years of age. The final practice puzzle had pieces about $3/4$ inch square, the size used in puzzles for older children and adults.

Strip-Cut Puzzles

Once you have successfully cut practice puzzles in all of the above sizes, it's time to move on to larger strip-cut puzzles, although you should really consider each puzzle you cut, no matter how large, a practice puzzle—an opportunity to hone your puzzle-cutting skills. There are four steps involved in making a strip-cut wooden jigsaw puzzle:

1. preparing the puzzle board,
2. marking out the puzzle board,
3. cutting the puzzle, and
4. finishing the puzzle.

Each of these steps will be discussed in some detail.

1. Preparing the Puzzle Board. The first step is selecting a picture. Since this involves some risk to the picture, and because there is much to be learned, do not use a picture of any particular value for your first puzzle. A photograph, picture postcard, greeting card, or calendar illustration will work nicely. The main criteria to be applied here are that the picture not be large, 6 by 8 inches at most, and that the image be interesting visually.

Trim the picture, using a sharp hobby knife, straightedge, and cutting mat. Leave a $1/8$-inch border on all sides of the picture. This border will allow for some placement errors in gluing the image to the puzzle board, as well as helping to ensure that no glue gets on the clamping cauls. If there is no border area as is often the case with photographs, about $1/8$ inch will be lost from each side of the picture. Keep the straightedge on the inside of the border when cutting so that any errors will occur in the border and not the picture.

Cut a piece of $1/4$-inch plywood the same size as the picture minus its borders. Examine both sides of the plywood to determine which side should be glued to the picture and which should be the back of the puzzle. Select the nicest-looking side for the back of the puzzle, since this is the side that will show. Normally, only minor differences will be found between the two sides of a sheet of plywood, usually in the color or grain pattern of the wood, and not serious defects. If there are major defects, such as dents, chips, or missing knots, either repair the defect with wood filler or use a different piece of plywood.

Sand the surfaces and edges of the plywood with a sanding block and abrasive paper. This is especially important for the side to be glued to the picture, since any unevenness here will telegraph or show through to the picture's surface, and will be plainly noticeable. It is essential that you wipe off all sawdust, because any sawdust remaining on the plywood surface when glued to the picture will show up as greatly magnified bumps. Place the piece of plywood on top of the picture to double-check that the border extends beyond the plywood on all four sides.

At this juncture, you need to decide whether you wish to apply a finish to the back of the puzzle. Refer to the section on wood finishes in chapter 1 for the pros and cons and how to apply the finish.

If you use tung oil, avoid getting any of it on the side of the puzzle to which the picture is to be glued, as it may prevent the glue from adhering properly. It might be wise to mask off the edges and front of the puzzle board with drafting tape to avoid this problem. The success of the entire puzzle-making process depends in large measure on the total adhesion of the picture to the plywood. If there are any gaps between the glued-on picture and the plywood, the puzzle board may be unusable. Therefore, it is important to use a gluing process that ensures against such failures, and although it is possible to apply the glue to the plywood puzzle board with a brush as you did with the practice puzzles, you will obtain much more satisfactory results with a small paint roller. For this process, you'll need

glue, a glue tray and tray support, a paint roller, clamping cauls, caul supports, C-clamps, and a stop block, as detailed in chapter 1.

Before applying any glue, test-clamp the piece of plywood between the two clamping cauls to make certain the cauls are the correct size, to determine the number of clamps you'll need, and to make sure you have everything you need close at hand so that you'll be able to clamp the glued plywood and picture as rapidly as possible. The moisture in the glue will cause the paper to expand, and if you delay the clamping process, the paper may form wrinkles that show after the glue has dried.

Assemble the caul support and place one of the 6-by-9-inch cauls upon it. Center the piece of plywood on top of this caul, and then lay a second 6-by-9-inch caul on top of the plywood to form a sandwich. Fit C-clamps around the periphery of the cauls, with two clamps spaced along each long side and one clamp centered at each end. Shift the caul support at a slight angle to accommodate the end clamps. When you are satisfied with the clamping arrangement, remove the clamps, opening them just sufficiently to slip easily off the cauls. Set the clamps aside in a convenient place.

Now place the puzzle picture face down on a clean piece of paper. Clamp the stop block to one end of the workbench with a C-clamp. Place the plywood puzzle board, back side down, so

Two cauls (smooth boards) and C-clamps are used when gluing the picture to a plywood puzzle board. The cauls help ensure that the surface of the picture is kept smooth while the glue sets.

that it butts up against the stop block. Set the glue tray on the workbench about 18 inches away from the end of the puzzle board, with the farthest end resting on the tray support. Pour a small amount of glue into the lower end of the tray. The slant of the tray will keep the glue in one end of the tray. Roll the paint roller into the glue, and then roll it back and forth on the bottom of the tray until it is evenly coated. Roll the glue-coated roller over the surface of the plywood from end to end and side to side. Rotate the piece of plywood 90 degrees and repeat the rolling of the glue onto the surface. If necessary, return the roller to the tray and recoat it with glue. Turn the piece of plywood another 90 degrees and repeat the rolling process to even out the coat of glue. The surface should have a fine, pebbly appearance with no streaks or gaps in the glue coating.

Carefully place the plywood, glue-side down, onto the back of the picture so that the borders are equal in width on all four sides. Now pick up the puzzle board and place it, face down and centered, on the surface of the caul already in position on top of the caul support. Place the second caul on top of the puzzle board, and then position and tighten the six C-clamps. Tighten the clamps gradually so that they exert equal pressure on the cauls. Leave the puzzle board clamped in the cauls for a half hour, then remove it and put it aside overnight while the glue sets.

After the puzzle board is clamped, clean the glue tray and roller, unless you intend to glue up some more puzzle boards at this time. Do not pour the left-

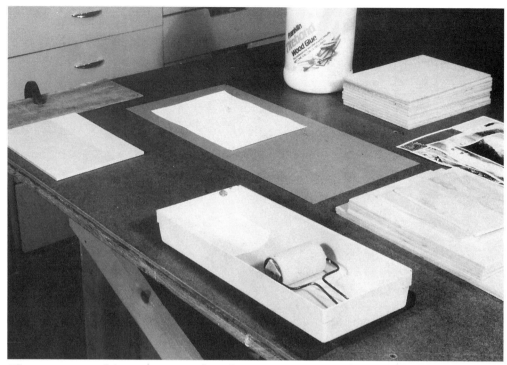

The arrangement of the equipment used in gluing pictures to puzzle boards facilitates the gluing process. From left to right, stop block, puzzle board, glue tray with roller, and tray raising block. The puzzle picture is face down on a clean piece of paper just behind the puzzle board.

over glue back into the original glue container; either discard it or pour it into a clean container. If the glue in the tray has become contaminated with sawdust or other debris, it would contaminate all the glue in the original container. Also, bacteria or yeast spores floating in the air may settle on the surface of the glue in the tray and find this an ideal medium in which to multiply. Over time, such contaminants can affect the strength of the glue bond. After a week or so, glue contaminated with bacteria or yeast will have an unpleasant, acrid odor.

Clean the glue from the tray and paint roller with soap and water. It will save a lot of effort to simply fill the tray with warm water and let it soak for an hour or so, and then use a scrub brush to remove any glue residue. If the paint roller cover is removable, rinse it well and immerse it in warm water in a small can or jar. Let it soak overnight, and you will find most of the glue residue in the bottom of the container. Rinse, then set the roller cover aside to drain and dry. If the roller cover is not removable, you'll have to soak the entire assembly to remove the glue.

After the glue on the puzzle board has set, remove it from the cauls and sand away the border strips with abrasive paper and a sanding block, gently rounding the edges and corner of the puzzle board. If traces of the border still appear after the picture has been sanded flush to the edges of the plywood, you'll have to reduce the size of the puzzle board to eliminate them. This is best done on a stationary disk or belt sander or a table saw. Be cautious when using a table saw; if the fence is not precisely parallel to the saw blade, the upward cutting of the teeth in back will make the edges of the puzzle ragged.

Next, examine the surface of the picture. Any gaps in the glue will show up as loose blisters in the paper. When you press down on these blisters with a finger, you can tell that there is air under them. These are hard defects to deal with. About the only practical remedy is to heat an ordinary household iron on the linen setting, place a clean piece of typing or similar paper on top of the puzzle, and iron the surface of the puzzle. Move the iron in a circular pattern, and exert quite a bit of pressure over the area of the blister. If this ironing is carried out within a day or so of gluing up the puzzle board, the glue will be thermoplastic and the remedy may work. In any event, it is worth a try. If you fail to eliminate the blister, you have little choice but to discard the puzzle board and begin anew. The spoiled puzzle board itself can be salvaged by dampening the picture surface with water until it comes free from the plywood, and then washing away the leftover glue. Let the plywood dry thoroughly before reusing it.

2. Marking Out. This process determines the number and size of the puzzle pieces. It is used primarily when making a puzzle by the strip-cutting method. Typically, strip-cut puzzle pieces will measure approximately $3/4$ inch on a side. This means that a puzzle measuring 6 by 9 inches would have ninety-six pieces, or eight strips cut into twelve pieces each.

You'll soon discover, however, that your puzzle boards seldom work out to be evenly divisible in either direction. In fact, if your first puzzle board measures exactly 5 by 8 inches, the 5-inch side divided by $3/4$ inch results in six divisions and a remainder of $1/2$ half inch. Similarly, the 8-inch side divided by $3/4$ inch results in ten divisions and a remainder of $1/2$ inch. The solution to the problem is to divide each side evenly, with widths as close to $3/4$ inch as practical. Five inches divided into six spaces would yield spaces .8333 inches wide, and 8 inches divided into ten spaces would yield spaces .8 inches wide. Both of these measurements would be difficult to mark out with an ordinary ruler, and the .8333 measurement would be difficult even with a ruler marked out in hundredths of an inch. One practical solution is to make a marking-out board for this task.

The marking-out board consists of a piece of cardboard or paper that can be any size larger than the puzzle board. A 12-by-12-inch square of white mat board will work well for this and subsequent puzzles. Using a pencil and starting at one edge of the cardboard, measure and draw a series of parallel lines 1/2 inch apart the length of the cardboard and across its entire width. Beginning at the upper left corner, number each line consecutively across the width of the cardboard, the corner itself being zero. Align one end of a 12-inch ruler exactly with the upper left corner of the cardboard, and move the other end of the ruler downward until it lines up exactly with line number sixteen. Draw a line along the edge of the ruler, and then extend this line to the opposite edge of the card-

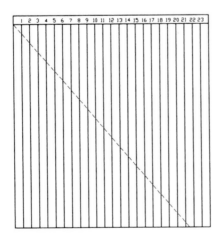

The marking-out board is used to space the strips in a strip-cut puzzle. It is made by drawing lines spaced 1/2 inch apart on a sheet of white cardboard.

board. The intersection of the vertical lines with this line should be exactly 3/4 inch apart. The completed marking-out board should look similar to the one shown in the illustration. To use the marking-out board, place one corner of the puzzle board directly on the intersection of a vertical line and the 3/4-inch line, and move the opposite end of the puzzle board up or down until it coincides with another vertical line as close as possible to the 3/4-inch line. If this alignment is above the 3/4-inch line, the spaces will be less than 3/4 inch wide. Conversely, if the alignment is below the 3/4-inch line, the spaces will be greater than 3/4 inch wide. If you want your puzzle pieces to be 3/4 inch or less, use the spacing above the line; to be wider, use the spacing below the line.

When marking out the puzzle board, do not make any marks on the picture surface, because they cannot be erased without damage to the picture. Instead, make small tick marks with a pencil on the edge of the puzzle board. These marks can be removed with the saw during the cutting process. For your first puzzle, you'll cut the strips the length of the puzzle board. Therefore, using the method just described, mark each end of the puzzle board with a pencil into segments 3/4 inch or wider. (You can use narrower widths later as you gain skill in strip-cutting puzzles.) Now you know where each of your strips should begin and end.

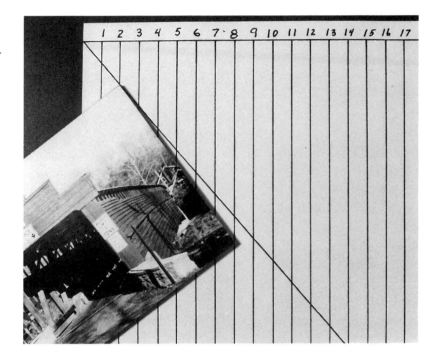

The puzzle board is placed upon the marking-out board at an angle to obtain even spacing for the desired number of strips to be cut.

Next, you need to determine where each strip should be cut crosswise to form the individual puzzle pieces. If you were to use the method just described, after you cut the first strip, there would be no marks remaining on the uncut portion of the puzzle board to guide the cutting of the puzzle pieces. As a consequence, you'll need to make and use a guide strip for this purpose.

Cut a 1^1/2-inch-wide strip of heavy paper (about the weight of a file folder) the exact length of the puzzle board. Lay this strip on the marking-out board so that it too is divided exactly into segments ^{3}/4 inch or wider. Now, holding the strip at the same angle, shift it to the left or right until both ends fall at

approximately the midpoint between two lines. This shifting of the strip is necessary so that when the guide strip is used in the cutting of interlocks, they will fall at the midpoint of each piece. Mark the strip at each point where its edge intersects a vertical line. Using a straightedge, draw parallel lines across the width of the strip at each mark. Lay the strip face down on a sheet of newspaper to protect the workbench surface and spray it with a light coat of repositionable spray adhesive. Remove the strip from the newspaper and set it aside for a few minutes so that the adhesive solvent can evaporate. This helps ensure that the adhesive will not transfer to the surface of the puzzle board.

3. Cutting the Puzzle. You are now ready to cut the puzzle. Fit the scroll saw with a #2/0 saw blade. Adjust the tension on the blade as described earlier. Lay the guide strip about 1/2 inch to the left of the first pair of marks, its ends flush with the ends of the puzzle board, and press it into place. Look at the first mark on the far end of the board to guide you in beginning the cut. Turn the saw on, align this mark with the saw blade, and begin your cut just as you did with the practice squares. Keep an eye on the guide strip, and as you approach the first mark, cut an interlock. This interlock can be to the right or left of the centerline, as you prefer. Continue cutting each interlock at the position shown by the guide strip. Alternate the interlocks from left to right and right to left as you proceed. Use the mark on the uncut end of the puzzle board as a guide for cutting the centerline, and try to exit the cut exactly on this mark, thereby removing it.

You probably will notice that in order to cut along the imaginary centerline parallel to the outer edge of the puz-

The guide strip, temporarily adhered to the puzzle board, helps you determine the spacing of the interlocks.

zle board, you have to turn the board slightly at an angle with the edge of the scroll saw table as you cut. This "out-of-squareness" of the saw usually is not a defect in the scroll saw itself, but, rather, can be traced to minor errors in the manufacture of the saw blades. Once you have a sense for the angle at which you need to feed the wood to cut a straight line, this oddity should not cause difficulty.

You can check whether the difficulty is with the blade or with the saw by drawing a straight line on a piece of ply-

wood. Cut along the line for several inches, and note the angle at which the wood has to be held to follow the line. Remove the saw blade and reclamp it in the scroll saw with the teeth pointing upward. Hold the piece of wood securely, turn on the saw, and cut another straight line, again noting the angle at which the wood has to be held to follow the line. If, during this second cut, you had to hold the wood at approximately the opposite angle than during the first cut, then the difficulty is with the blade. If you still

have to hold the wood at the same or a similar angle as with the first cut, then the saw is out of alignment and needs to be adjusted following the manufacturer's instructions.

After you have cut the first strip, set it aside and repeat the process until you have cut all the strips from the puzzle board. You may be tempted at this point to dispense with the guide strip and use the interlocks already cut as guides for the interlocks in subsequent strips. For a small puzzle this generally will work, but as the puzzles you are cutting become larger, errors in the spacing of the interlocks may compound to the point that some will be too far apart and some too close together. To continue to use the guide strip, simply peel it off the puzzle board and move it over for the next strip. When you are finished with the guide strip, write the length of the strip on it, punch a hole in one end, and hang it on a nail for use

In the strip-cutting process, the puzzle board is first cut into a series of interlocking strips, and then the strips are cut into the individual puzzle pieces.

in cutting other puzzle boards of the same length. The adhesive on it will remain tacky for a long time.

When cutting the interlocks on the strips, you may inadvertently cut two consecutive interlocks on the same side of the centerline. This does not pose a problem of any kind, since you could, if desired, put all of the interlocks on the same side. The interlocks would still work and the puzzle would still be a puzzle. If you want to get back in phase with the other interlocks, however, you need to cut a third interlock on the same side. The next interlock then will be back in phase.

Once you have sawn all of the strips, each one needs to be cut into individual pieces following the process described in the practice section. Your major concerns here are deciding where the centerline for each crosscut should fall and on which side of the centerline each interlock should be cut. It may be helpful to review the various puzzle shapes illustrated earlier. You may prefer the shape of one piece over another. If so, cut more of those pieces and less of the others; there are no rules here, and it's up to your personal preference. Also, you can make some of the pieces larger or smaller than others if desired.

As you are cutting the puzzle, be alert for any indication that the picture is not completely glued down to the plywood, such as an edge of the picture lifting off the plywood as it passes the blade. As soon as you finish cutting such a piece, set it apart from the other pieces. Examine the pieces surrounding this one; there are probably adjacent pieces on which the picture also is loose. Set any such pieces apart as well. When you have finished cutting the puzzle, reglue those on which the picture is loose with a very fine-pointed paintbrush or a toothpick. As you apply glue to the plywood, do not bend the loose portion of the picture too far back, or you will create a crease in the paper that will be visible after it has been glued. Hold the glued portion of the piece between the thumb and forefinger for a few seconds, then carefully wipe away any glue from the edges of the piece. If you get glue on the surface of the picture, wipe it away with a damp sponge. Be extra careful when doing this to avoid damaging the surface.

There are several other defects that may develop before or during the cutting of the puzzle. The first of these may have occurred during the gluing process. If any debris such as sawdust or hair became embedded in the glue, it will result in an obvious magnified bump in the surface of the picture. Should this happen, do not try to crush the bump by applying excessive clamping pressure. This may result in an even more obvious defect in the surface of the picture. Instead, when cutting the puzzle, try to saw right through the bump. Though this will not totally eliminate the bump, it will make it much less noticeable.

"Dreibelbis Bridge," the completed strip-cut puzzle. It measures 5 by 7 1/2 inches and has 60 pieces.

Particles also may have been trapped between the surface of the paper and the clamping caul during the gluing up of the puzzle, or there may have been defects in the surface of the caul. When glue is applied, the paper becomes quite soft and is easily imprinted with anything caught between it and another surface. Nothing can be done to correct this kind of surface defect. Just be more scrupulous when gluing up the next puzzle board.

By far the most serious error occurs if you scratch or otherwise mar the surface of the picture. Here, prevention is the best cure. Be careful whenever handling a picture or a puzzle board with the pic-

ture glued on it. Store your pictures and puzzle boards with clean slip sheets of paper between them. Be careful when placing a puzzle board face down on any surface, first ensuring that there is nothing on that surface that could scratch the picture. If you are using your scroll saw with the hold-down foot in place, examine and remove any nicks or scratches on the bottom of the foot that could damage the picture, and set the hold-down foot sufficiently above the puzzle board so that it does not ride on the surface of the picture when the puzzle is being cut.

If there is a scratch in the surface of the picture, you can try to eliminate it by sawing along it when cutting the puzzle. If that doesn't work, complete the making of the puzzle anyway, or discard the puzzle board and all of the pieces already cut. One other alternative, although it's only occasionally successful, unless you are a skilled artist, is to attempt to hide the scratch with colored pencils, marking pens, watercolor paint, acrylic paint, pastel crayons, or other coloring materials. The difficulty is in finding a coloring agent that will adhere to the surface of the picture and match the various colors and textures of the scratch without staining or otherwise being as noticeable as the scratch itself. It certainly is worth a try, however, and may allow you to save an otherwise spoiled puzzle board.

4. Finishing the Puzzle. Once all the pieces have been cut, assemble the puzzle in preparation for sanding the backs of the puzzle pieces. With your practice puzzles, you sanded the back of the individual pieces on a sanding board. It is difficult to do so without also sanding the tips of your fingers, however, and there's a more sophisticated method to get rid of the unwanted loose wood fibers using a finishing frame. The finishing frame consists of a square or rectangular panel of hardboard or plywood with narrow strips of wood glued to two adjacent edges. Directions for constructing the finishing frame and holder are given in chapter 7.

The assembled puzzle is turned upside down onto the surface of the finishing frame and then slid into the corner formed by the two strips of wood. The easiest way to turn a puzzle over is to slip the puzzle onto a piece of stiff cardboard slightly larger than the puzzle itself, place a second piece of cardboard on top of the puzzle, pick the assembly up as if it were a sandwich, and turn it over. The puzzle then can be slid onto the finishing frame. The opposite corner of the puzzle is held with a thin piece of plywood with a V notch cut in one end. By pressing the puzzle into the corner of the two wood strips, you can hold the puzzle quite securely with one hand while you sand the puzzle back. Use 150-grit abrasive paper and a sanding block, and sand using a circular motion followed by a straight-line motion. You might want to rotate the puzzle on the sanding frame several times as you sand, to remove as much of the loose wood fibers as possible.

Now you need to remove the wood dust from between the puzzle pieces and back and front of the puzzle. This is made much easier with the use of a cleaning screen. The cleaning screen consists of hardware cloth stretched across a wooden frame. Directions for constructing a cleaning screen are also given in chapter 7. After you've sanded the back of the assembled puzzle, place the cleaning screen over it, screen side down, and use a vacuum cleaner with a crevice tool to vacuum the surface of the puzzle through the screen. This will remove most of the dust from the back and the spaces between the puzzle

The sanding of the back of a puzzle to remove tear-out after it has been cut is facilitated by the use of a finishing frame, hold-down, and padded sanding block.

pieces. Turn the puzzle board over using the procedure described above, and slide it back onto the finishing frame. Again, place the cleaning screen on top of the puzzle, and vacuum the face of the puzzle. You can also use the cleaning screen to clean the puzzle pieces immediately after they are cut. Pour the pieces into the screen and shake it gently so that the loose sawdust falls through the screen and onto your workbench top or into a waste receptacle. These cleaning processes should remove practically all dust from the puzzle.

Undoubtedly, by now you will have noticed several things you should have done differently when making your first strip-cut puzzle. Some of the puzzle pieces may be poorly cut or fail to interlock. The picture may not look as interesting as you thought it would now that it's cut into puzzle pieces. The surface of the picture may be uneven because the glue was not applied properly. The only way to improve your skills in puzzle making is by making more puzzles. Therefore, repeat the above procedures, using pictures the same size or perhaps larger than the first one, to make additional strip-cut puzzles until you feel comfortable with the process and can obtain satisfactory results.

The cleaning screen can be placed on top of the puzzle to hold the pieces in place while it is vacuumed to remove dust created when cutting the puzzle pieces and when sanding the back of the puzzle.

Large Strip-Cut Puzzles

When your strip-cut puzzles become larger in size, you may notice a degrading of the outer edges of the puzzle board opposite the strip being cut. As you hold this edge of the puzzle board with your right hand and turn the board as you cut the interlocks, your hand is continually shifting its position. This results in the wearing away of the surface of the puzzle's picture on this edge of the puzzle board. This wear shows up as a white, ever-widening line along the edge of the puzzle and is especially noticeable if the paper is lightweight, as is the case with color photocopies. To minimize this wear, either protect the surface of the picture with a coat of paste wax to serve as a buffer between your hands and the surface of the paper, or change the way you cut the puzzle to reduce the amount

of handling of the outer edges of the puzzle board.

Use a white paste wax to protect the surface of the paper; unlike yellow waxes, it will not alter the colors of the picture. Apply the wax in a thin layer with a clean, soft cloth following the manufacturer's directions. Heavy layers of wax create obvious ridges when polished. When the wax has had time to dry, buff it with another soft cloth or a lamb's wool pad. Before cutting the puzzle, allow the wax to dry for several hours so there is time for the solvents to evaporate.

The second way of protecting the puzzle edges from wear and tear is to change the way you cut the puzzle. After you've cut the initial strip from one edge of the puzzle board, turn the board 180 degrees and cut the second strip from the opposite, uncut edge. By repeating this process for each strip, you minimize the wear and tear on any one strip.

As you progress to cutting larger and larger puzzles, you'll reach a point where it becomes physically difficult to turn the puzzle board as you are cutting the interlocks. As you turn the puzzle board, you may have to stand in a very awkward position so that the corners will clear your body. To overcome this problem, you can make an initial cut right down the center of the puzzle board, cutting interlocks as you go, thus dividing the board into two interlocking halves. Following this cut, you can then cut each of these halves in half perpendicular to the original cut, resulting in the puzzle board being divided into four interlocking quarters. Once the puzzle board has been divided this way, you can cut each of the four sections into strips and puzzle pieces as if they were individual puzzle boards.

Only through practice can you become skillful at making wooden jigsaw puzzles, so make a variety of strip-cut puzzles in a range of sizes within the capacity of your scroll saw before moving on to other techniques.

Large puzzle boards are difficult to handle when cutting. Dividing them into smaller, interlocking sections helps minimize this problem.

Three

Cutting Puzzles with a Fretsaw

IN THE YEARS BEFORE WORLD WAR I and again during the Great Depression before World War II, jigsaw puzzle mania swept the nation. Thousands of puzzles were cut, thousands were sold, and thousands were rented from puzzle libraries just as you rent videotapes today. Many of these puzzles were wooden and were cut by hand by amateur puzzle cutters using nothing more complex than a fretsaw and fretsaw table. In fact, throughout the history of the wooden jigsaw puzzle, there have been puzzle cutters who use only this type of saw to cut their puzzles.

To learn to cut wooden jigsaw puzzles with a fretsaw, it's best to start with small practice squares as you did when learning to strip-cut with a scroll saw. You'll need a fretsaw, a fretsaw table, a saw blade, and a stool for sitting while cutting the puz-

zle. Directions for constructing a fretsaw table are given in chapter 7. Although fretsaws are available with throats as deep as 24 inches, you are better off starting with one with a 10- or 12-inch throat. The saw blades you use should be the same as you used with the scroll saw, except perhaps a little larger, at least a #1 or even a #2.

With the teeth pointing downward toward the handle and outward away from the saw frame, fasten the lower end of a scroll saw blade in the blade clamp nearest the handle of the fretsaw. Align its upper end with the clamp on the opposite end of the saw frame. Hold the saw against the edge of the workbench and insert the blade in the upper clamp. Press the saw frame against the bench and tighten the clamp. This will give tension to the blade. Release the pressure on the saw frame and check the blade tension by plucking it just as you did with the scroll saw. You should hear a musical sound. If the sound is dull and unmusical, release the blade from the upper clamp and repeat the tensioning process.

Clamp the fretsaw table to the top of your workbench, and seat yourself in front and slightly to the left of it. Place your first practice square on top of the fretsaw table, with the side where you intend to begin sawing extended just slightly over the V notch. Hold the saw

with the handle pointing downward, the frame of the saw just alongside your upper arm with the blade resting lightly on the edge of the plywood where the initial cut is to begin. Start moving the saw frame up and down in a vertical motion. Hold the saw so that its blade is perpendicular to the piece of plywood from side to side and front to back. This is essential to the successful cutting of the puzzle. Move the fretsaw up and down at a moderate speed (about four strokes per second) and press the practice square into the blade with your left hand. You also

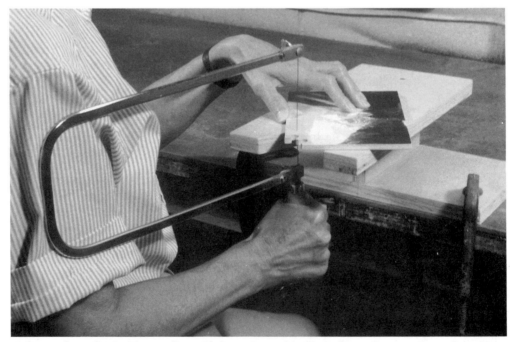

A fretsaw frame fitted with a scroll saw blade can be used in place of a scroll saw or jigsaw for cutting wooden jigsaw puzzles. Note how the saw is held in a vertical position when being used. This helps ensure that the edges of the puzzle pieces are cut square with respect to their upper and lower surfaces.

have to hold the puzzle board down with your left hand at the same time. This sounds complicated, but you'll soon master the process. You and the fretsaw are the "scroll saw." The wood moves into the saw rather than the saw moving into the wood. Most of the difficulties encountered in using a fretsaw are because this principle is violated or the blade is not kept vertical.

As you approach a curve—for example, the knob of an interlock—keep the fretsaw blade moving up and down in a steady rhythm, and feed the practice square into the blade very slowly. The blade should not jam in the saw cut. If it does, you probably were trying to cut the curve too rapidly. When you have cut the practice square into four puzzle pieces, try assembling them. The pieces should go together easily. If you have difficulty fitting any of the pieces together, the pieces likely have been cut at an angle. This means that you did not keep the saw blade perpendicular to the puzzle board when cutting. Should this be the case, cut another square, and then another, until you find a natural sawing rhythm and speed that produces clean, square-cut puzzle pieces with smooth, flowing lines.

Treat broken fretsaw blades in pretty much the same way as broken scroll saw blades. With a fretsaw, since you control the speed of the saw, you can more easily negotiate reentry into the saw cut.

First study where the break occurred, however, and if you think it would be better to make a crosswise cut or to begin from the opposite end of the cut, then do so.

Once you feel that you and your fretsaw can work together as a team, try cutting a small picture puzzle. The limiting factor in the size of the puzzle you can cut with your fretsaw, as with the scroll saw, is the depth of its throat. A fretsaw with a 12-inch throat can only accommodate a puzzle about $10^1/2$ inches square.

After you have cut the puzzle, assemble it, setting aside any pieces that bind or that fit only if put in place in one way. When you have finished putting the puzzle together, sand the edge of each set-aside piece where it binds until it will fit easily into place. Remove excess wood from the bottom edge of the piece rather than the top edge. This may require sanding the mating piece rather than the one you thought was binding. In this way, any gap produced from the sanding will be on the bottom of the puzzle and will not be noticeable when the puzzle is assembled. When all of the puzzle pieces fit together easily, finish the puzzle as described in the previous chapter.

Learning to cut wooden jigsaw puzzles with a fretsaw may seem to some a waste of energy, but you may find it a very satisfying experience. You certainly can rest secure in the knowledge that your puzzles really are hand-cut.

Four

Advanced Puzzle-Cutting Techniques

A S YOU HAVE BY NOW DISCOVERED, the making of wooden jigsaw puzzles involves a wide range of tools and materials combined with a number of processes to produce a finished puzzle. Now that you have acquired the fundamental skills needed for puzzle cutting, you're ready to learn some advanced puzzle-cutting techniques that will enable you to make increasingly more interesting and challenging wooden jigsaw puzzles. In this chapter, we will explore ways to enhance the visual interest of individual jigsaw puzzle pieces, to alter the overall shape of the puzzle board, and to create three-dimensional puzzles. Try making at least one puzzle using each of the techniques described. You then can decide which kinds of puz-

zles you most enjoy making and which kinds your friends and family most enjoy assembling.

For most puzzle enthusiasts, the more difficult a puzzle is to put together, the more challenging it is—assuming, of course, that the puzzle provides visual interest as well. After you've made a number of strip-cut puzzles, you will become aware that, generally speaking, there are not many variations to the shape of the puzzle pieces. Such predictability of shapes leads to puzzles that are relatively easy to assemble. The experienced puzzle enthusiast will simply sort the strip-cut puzzle pieces by those that are obviously edge pieces, assemble the border of the puzzle, and then sort the remaining pieces by color and shape for the final assembly. This does not imply that all strip-cut puzzles are necessarily easy to assemble nor that all of them are composed of uninteresting pieces. At a conference on puzzle cutting some years ago, I heard disparaging remarks about strip-cut puzzles. I turned to a fellow puzzle cutter who had been making jigsaw puzzles for a number of years and asked her, "Are strip-cut puzzles really bad?" To which she replied, "Not if they have interesting pieces." Therefore, it is up to you to devise some means for making the strip-cut pieces more interesting.

More Adventuresome Strip-Cut Puzzles

One way you can achieve interest in a strip-cut puzzle is to depart from the straight lines you have been using to lines that change direction, curving first this way and then that. If you use curved, interlocking lines to cut strips that run the length of the puzzle board, and then cut similar curved, interlocking lines across the width of the puzzle, the pieces, though still being strip-cut, would have shapes that vary considerably from one another.

To try this approach, mark out a prepared puzzle board to indicate where strips should begin and end. You'll need a guide strip, at least for cutting the two outer strips. Begin cutting the first strip, but do not cut straight toward the opposite end of the puzzle board. Rather,

introduce a mild outward or inward curve until you reach the point where the first interlock needs to be cut. Cut the interlock, and then, as you emerge from it, resume cutting a gentle curve. As you approach the second interlock, begin to reverse the direction of the curve, cut the interlock, and continue the path of the curve just begun. Continue cutting in this fashion until you reach the end of the strip. Try to vary not only the direction of the curves but also their length and depth to produce a pleasant, undulating line. Vary the placement of the interlocks as well. Instead of alternating them first to the right and then to the left, cut some of the interlocks so that two or more in a row face the same direction. Try to introduce as many variations into the strip-cutting process as possible so as to achieve continually varying and nonpredictable puzzle pieces.

Now cut the strip on the opposite edge of the puzzle board in a similar fashion. After cutting the second strip, set the guide strip aside, and cut the remaining strips so that the spaces between them at times become wider and at other times narrower. In so doing, you'll find that the spacing of the interlocks gradually will change, adding interest to the puzzle. Be careful, however, not to place two adjacent interlocks so close together that there is no room for crosscutting the strip.

When you have finished cutting all the strips, assemble them together, turn the

Strip-cut puzzles need not lack visual interest, as demonstrated by this puzzle with curved pieces. The puzzle, "Wetzlar, Germany," measures 6 7/8 by 9 1/2 inches and has 108 pieces.

assembled puzzle board upside down on the finishing frame, and sand any splinters from the back. Brush away all excess sawdust and then apply strips of 3/4- or 1-inch-wide, low-tack drafting tape across the width of the back of the puzzle board, pulling the strips tightly against one another. Begin at one end of the puzzle board and continue to the opposite end, so that the entire back of the puzzle board is covered with drafting tape.

Cut a piece of cardboard about the weight of a tablet back to the same size as the puzzle board. Protect your work surface with newspaper, then apply a coat of spray adhesive to the cardboard, being certain to cover it completely. Now lower the puzzle board, taped side down, onto the piece of cardboard. Be precise; adhesion is instant, so any errors made in positioning the board on the cardboard cannot be corrected. Turn the board over and rub the surface of the cardboard thoroughly to ensure that it sticks to the drafting tape. Follow the directions on the spray can for clean-up.

Turn the puzzle board right side up. All of the strips should remain together, and you should be able to cut the puzzle board into a series of strips running the width of the puzzle board. The cardboard will provide rigidity when crosscutting the puzzle strips. Cut these strips with smooth, undulating curves like the ones you cut earlier, with the interlocks falling between the strips. Some of the pieces will be quite small and narrow; others will swell out and be rather wide. Be on the lookout for pieces where the interlocks might become too close together inside a piece; here, cut the interlock so that it extends into the opposite puzzle piece. By cutting the strips across the width of the puzzle as well as down its length, they will flow into one another to create a nice rhythm—something you could not easily achieve by cutting each strip into pieces separately.

When you have finished cutting the puzzle, separate the pieces from one another, removing the drafting tape at the same time. Assemble the pieces and finish the back of the puzzle board, then examine it carefully, noting which pieces are most and which are least interesting. In subsequent puzzles, try to plan your cutting so that you increase the number of interesting pieces and reduce the number of uninteresting ones.

Puzzles Without Interlocks

Many jigsaw puzzles of the late eighteenth and early nineteenth centuries were sliced-cut—that is, they were cut into pieces using straight or curved lines with no interlocks. The absence of interlocks makes a puzzle much more challenging, not only because of the difficulty of holding the pieces while assembling the puzzle, but also because these puzzles lack the clues provided by interlocks. Instead of looking for a puzzle piece with a knob on one edge that will fit the socket of another, you have to use the shapes, colors, and texture of the pieces to put the puzzle together.

Such a puzzle is quite easy to make. Select a small, prepared puzzle board, and cut it into a series of strips with undulat-

Some puzzles, such as sliced-cut puzzles, do not have interlocks to hold the pieces together. The first step in making such a puzzle is to cut the puzzle board into strips.

Once the puzzle board has been cut into strips, the strips are then cut into individual pieces. The puzzle shown, "Alpine View," measures 5 by 7 inches and has 54 pieces.

ing curves similar to those cut in the preceding puzzle but without interlocks. Sand both back edges of each strip to remove any splinters. After all of the strips have been cut and sanded, align them in the order in which they were cut. Following the instructions for the preceding puzzle, tape them together, cut a piece of cardboard the same size as the puzzle, apply a coat of spray adhesive, and place the taped back of the puzzle board on top of the cardboard.

Then turn the reassembled puzzle board over and cut it into curved strips crosswise to the strips already cut, varying the curves to produce interesting-shaped pieces. After all of the puzzle pieces are cut, remove the tape and cardboard and assemble the pieces. Sand any tear-out from the back of the puzzle. You may find it difficult to hold the puzzle together while sanding, since there are no interlocks to join the individual pieces to one another. Slip the puzzle onto the finishing frame upside down, and then use two narrow strips of 1/4-inch plywood rather than the hold-down to hold the puzzle in place while sanding.

Tray Puzzles

A tray puzzle is a variation of the noninterlocking puzzle that eliminates most of the problems associated with assembly.[1] The outer edges of the puzzle board form the border of the tray, providing a frame within which to assemble the puzzle.

To construct a tray puzzle, select a prepared puzzle board that has an unfinished back, and decide on an approximate width to make the border. The smaller the puzzle, the narrower the border should be. It's a matter of what looks best. Somewhere between $1/2$ and $3/4$ inch would be appropriate for a medium-size puzzle. For a tray puzzle the size of a postcard, the border should be much narrower, perhaps $1/4$ to $3/8$ inch wide. For a very large puzzle, the border might be 1 inch or wider.

Once you have determined an appropriate width for the border, drill a $1/16$-inch diameter entry hole through the puzzle board at about that distance in from the edge, somewhere near the midpoint of one of the sides. Try to select a spot where there is quite a bit of visual activity and where one of the strips will be cut—for example, among the leaves of a tree—so that the hole will be less noticeable in the finished puzzle.

Fasten a #2/0 blade in the lower

clamp of the scroll saw with its upper end aligned with the upper clamp. Slide the puzzle board, bottom side down, across the upper end of the blade until it lines up with the hole just drilled. This may require some bending of the blade; do so gently so that you don't break it. Lower the puzzle board until it rests on the saw's table. Move the puzzle board as necessary to allow the blade to stand perpendicular to the top of the board. Fasten the upper end of the blade in the upper clamp of the saw and adjust the tension.

Turn the puzzle board until it is aligned with the saw blade in the direction you wish to begin cutting the border. Then turn the saw motor on and cut the border. It's easier to cut the border using gently curving lines rather than straight lines, and the corners should be rounded. As you reach the fourth side, plan ahead so that when the cut reaches the starting point (the entry hole), the meeting of the two lines will be smooth and continuous.

Turn the saw motor off. Loosen the upper blade clamp and remove the border and interior piece from the saw table. Sand the bottom edges of the border to remove loose wood fibers and splinters, then set the border aside.

Cut a piece of cardboard the same size as the interior piece of the puzzle board and temporarily put it aside. Cut the interior portion of the puzzle board into strips without interlocks, as described for the previous puzzle, tape the strips

---

1. Steve Malavolta, "Jigsaw Puzzles," *Fine Woodworking* 60 (September–October 1986): 66–69. Other types of tray puzzles are also discussed in this article.

Sliced-cut puzzles are difficult to assemble because they lack interlocks to hold the pieces together. A tray puzzle minimizes this difficulty by providing a frame to contain the puzzle as it is being assembled. The frame is formed by cutting around the outside edges of the puzzle board with the scroll saw. You'll have to drill a small hole in the puzzle board through which to thread the saw blade.

together, and fasten them to the piece of cardboard. Cut the reassembled puzzle board into crosswise strips.

Place the border on a stiff piece of cardboard slightly larger than the border itself. Remove the tape and cardboard from the puzzle pieces, and assemble them inside the border. You'll find that the border serves well to hold the pieces in place. Once you have assembled the puzzle, pick it up with the piece of cardboard, turn it over as described in chapter 2 for strip-cut puzzles, place it on the finishing frame, and sand the back of the puzzle. Then, with the aid of a cleaning

screen (see chapter 2), vacuum the puzzle to remove the sawdust.

Now remove the puzzle pieces from within the border and put them aside. Cut a piece of plywood about 1/8 inch longer and wider than the border to serve as the back of the tray. Prepare cauls and clamps for gluing as you would for gluing a picture to a puzzle board. Using a small brush, apply a coat of glue to the back of the border along all four edges. Keep the glue away from the inside edges of the border to avoid having glue squeeze out on the inside of the tray. Then place the border on top of the back piece and

The puzzle tray is formed by gluing the frame to a piece of plywood with the same outside dimensions as the frame.

clamp it between the cauls. After the glue has set, trim the back to the edges of the border with a table saw or stationary sanding machine. Sand the sides to remove any sharp edges. Check the inside of the tray, and if any glue is present, remove it with a sharp chisel. Reassemble the puzzle, and it is finished.

Still More Variations

If you find noninterlocking puzzles interesting to make and fun to assemble, you may want to explore other techniques for cutting them. You'll find many such puzzles illustrated in Williams's *History of Jigsaw Puzzles.* Study them and try cutting variations of those that interest you. You can also experiment by simply cutting a puzzle board into pieces without first

cutting it into strips. Try to vary the shapes, but avoid making pieces too small or too large so as to appear out of keeping with the rest of the puzzle pieces. You can usually cut a piece that is too large into two pieces, but there's no remedy for a piece that's too small.

If you like making tray puzzles but want to move into puzzle shapes that are more free-form, then follow the above instructions for cutting the border and making the tray, but instead of cutting the interior portion of the puzzle board into strips, cut it into shapes as you desire.

If cutting free-form puzzles engages you but you'd like your puzzles to be more traditional in form, there is a simple solution to help hold them together without a tray: Cut the edge pieces so

"Dreibelbis Bridge." The pieces of a strip-cut puzzle typically measure approximately three-fourths of an inch on a side.

"Alpine View." The absence of interlocks in the sliced-cut form makes for a more challenging puzzle.

"Alex and Schatzi." A puzzle with irregular edges is formed by cutting along the outlines of the major objects of the picture and discarding the remainder of the border. Photograph for puzzle picture by Susan Kern.

"Wetzlar, Germany." Using curved rather than straight lines to cut strips creates pieces with an interesting variety of shapes.

"Pennsylvania." The width of the border on a tray puzzle should be determined by the size of the puzzle—the smaller the puzzle, the narrower the border should be.

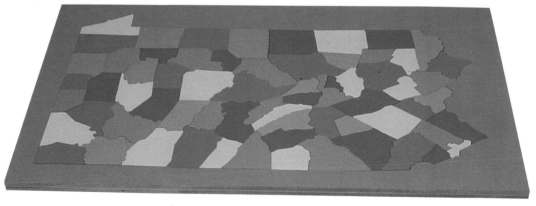

"Finger-Painting I." The tray puzzle is a good solution to many of the problems associated with assembly of noninterlocking puzzles. Painting for puzzle picture by Allison Kern.

"Kutztown Depot." A puzzle's level of difficulty can be increased through the use of line cutting, which is simply cutting along a straight line of an image in the puzzle picture. This forms pieces that are easily confused with edge pieces.

"Crater Lake." For free-form pieces, cut the puzzle board into pieces without first cutting it into strips.

"Watches I." Figure pieces should be about one and one-half inches in any direction. Anything larger will overwhelm the puzzle; anything smaller may be too difficult to cut or too easy to break. Collage for puzzle picture by William W. Hummel.

After the tray is completed, the interior portion of the puzzle board is cut into pieces using the slice-cut process. When all of the pieces have been cut, the puzzle is assembled inside the tray. This tray puzzle, "Finger-Painting I," is from a painting by Allison Kern. It measures 7 1/2 by 10 1/2 inches and has 104 pieces.

that they interlock with one another, and cut the interior of the puzzle into free-form pieces, interlocking or not, as you prefer. There are two ways to cut a puzzle with an interlocking border and free-form pieces. First, you can begin at some point on the outer edge of the puzzle—a corner, perhaps—and cut one interlocking piece after another until all of the edges have been cut. These edge pieces should not be so precisely defined as those of a strip-cut puzzle, because they would conflict visually with the shape of the interior pieces. Try to cut these edge pieces so that each, although interlock-

ing, has the fluid appearance of a free-form puzzle piece. Once you've cut the edge pieces, cut the interior of the puzzle into free-form pieces. It's good to have a number of these interior pieces also interlock to help hold the puzzle together as it's being assembled.

The second way to cut such puzzles is to begin anywhere on the edge of the puzzle, cut the first piece with an interlock on each end, and then work your way toward the interior of the puzzle by cutting pieces around and beyond this first piece. You're essentially nibbling away at the puzzle, cutting each piece

Instead of cutting the puzzle board into strips and the strips into pieces, you can cut it into free-form pieces, as shown here, in a kind of "nibbling" process.

into a shape best suited and most appropriate in terms of the pieces surrounding it. You'll need to exercise some care as the puzzle becomes smaller and smaller to avoid ending up with a piece that is too large but does not lend itself to being cut into two pieces. The smaller the puzzle board becomes, the greater the likelihood that it may be pulled from your grip by the saw blade, so keep a firm grip on it. As you approach the edge of the puzzle, keep in mind that you'll need to create an interlock just before you end the cut, thus forming another edge piece. Edge pieces can be almost any size, and some

of them may be cut with very little, even none, of the edge showing, while others may include considerably more of the edge. You can even eliminate a corner piece, if you wish, simply by cutting the adjacent edge pieces so that they intersect at an angle at the corner.

Line Cutting

Many puzzle enthusiasts begin the assembly of a puzzle by sorting out the edge pieces. Consequently, one good way to thwart them in this approach—and add challenge to a puzzle—is to employ the technique of line cutting. In line cutting, you simply cut along the edge of some image in the puzzle picture such as the roofline of a building. The areas on both sides of the line cut are then treated as if they were edge pieces. If the edge along which the line cut was made is straight, the person assembling the puzzle is apt to confuse these pieces with genuine edge pieces. Line cutting may also serve to separate adjacent areas of color and texture making it much more difficult to determine where a specific piece of the puzzle fits. You can also use line cutting to cut around a small area of a puzzle, such as the interior of a window, and then discard that part of the puzzle. The person assembling the puzzle will search and search for the missing puzzle pieces before realizing that they're not included with the puzzle. Do not get so carried away by the technique, however, that you unintentionally cut the puzzle into two puzzles.

Puzzles with Irregular Edges

Irregular edge cutting is another technique resulting in puzzles that are a challenge to assemble. A puzzle with irregular edges is formed by cutting along the outlines of major objects in the picture and discarding the remainder of the border. In some puzzles with irregular edges, there are no straight edge pieces at all. As with line cutting, puzzles with irregular edges are more difficult to assemble than

Line cutting involves cutting puzzle pieces by following a well-defined separation between two or more colors or edges in a puzzle picture. One result of line cutting is to form more "edge" pieces than there are edges in the puzzle. Since most puzzle enthusiasts sort out the edge pieces and put them together first, additional puzzle pieces with edges make the puzzle more challenging. The roof line of the "Kutztown Depot" provides an opportunity for such line cutting.

Additional interest can be intro-
duced to a puzzle by cutting
away a portion following some
obvious features in the puzzle
picture, thereby reducing the num-
ber of straight-sided edge pieces.
This irregular-edged puzzle,
"Alex and Schatzi," from a pho-
tograph by Susan Kern, was
formed by cutting along the out-
lines of the dog and the boy. It
measures about 7 by 7 1/4 inches
and has 52 pieces.

the traditional rectangular
puzzles: This is the major purpose of the technique.

Figure Pieces

When puzzle pieces are cut to
look like other objects—an
animal, a bird, a star, a letter of
the alphabet—they are called *figure pieces.*
Figure pieces have played a major role in
the history of jigsaw puzzles. In the days
when wooden jigsaw puzzles were cut
commercially, the cutters were expected
to include a minimum number of figure
pieces in each puzzle.[2] Today many puzzle makers also include figure pieces in
their puzzles.

Most figure pieces are cut using a pattern. Though it is possible to cut figure
pieces free-hand, there is considerable
risk that they may not turn out as

planned. Therefore, if you want to experiment with the use of figure pieces in
your puzzles, you should make some patterns. There are numerous sources of
images to use for figure pieces: children's
books, clip art, fretsaw patterns, and
books on design. You can enlarge or
reduce the image to any size desired on a
photocopying machine. A typical figure
piece usually should not exceed $1^{1/2}$
inches in any direction. Larger than this,
they will overwhelm the other pieces in
the puzzle; smaller than this, they may be
too difficult to cut or too easy to break.
Keep in mind that the piece will need to

---

2. Williams, *History and Price Guide,* 35.

be cut with the scroll saw and that it should not have any long, narrow projections that might break off. It is usually not possible to cut features, such as eyes, in the interior of the figure piece. Think of the figure piece as a silhouette.

Once you've found the images you want to use as figure pieces, the next step is to transform them into patterns. You may want to use some of your figure pieces in more than one puzzle, so make copies of them by cutting a pattern of the figure piece from stiff cardboard and then

tracing around this pattern with a pencil or pen onto to a piece of typing paper. Then cut out the tracing, leaving a border of 1/4 inch or more. Alternatively, you could simply make a photocopy of your pattern each time you want to use it. This would be very wasteful, however, because the image would occupy only a small portion of the paper on which it is printed. It would be better to either make photocopies of all your figure pieces or make multiple copies of the same figure piece, cut them out, and glue them to a

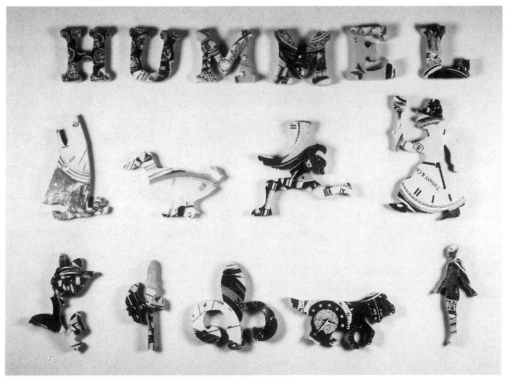

Many puzzle cutters like to introduce figure pieces, like the ones shown, in their jigsaw puzzles. Figure pieces can be animals, letters, everyday objects—even imaginary objects.

single sheet of paper. You could then photocopy this "master" any time you wanted to use the patterns. This is what I do when making patterns for signature pieces (discussed later in the chapter).

After you've copied your patterns for figure pieces, their backs need to be coated with a low-tack, repositionable spray adhesive so that the pattern can be adhered to the puzzle and then removed without damaging the surface of the picture. Place the paper pattern with the figure facing down on a sheet of newspaper and apply the spray adhesive to the back of the pattern. Remove the pattern from the newspaper and allow it to set for a few minutes until most of the solvents in the adhesive have evaporated. Then pick up the pattern and place it on the face of the puzzle board where that figure piece is to be cut. Rub the pattern gently to ensure that it adheres to the puzzle board. If your figure pieces are grouped together on a single sheet of paper, you can apply the adhesive to the whole sheet, wait for the solvents to evaporate, and then lay it adhesive side down on a piece of waxed paper or the glossy side of a piece of freezer wrap. This backing paper will protect the adhesive from dust and dirt when stored. Whenever you want one of the patterns on the piece of paper, simply cut it out with a pair of scissors, peel off the backing paper, and adhere it in place on the puzzle board. The adhesive will remain

tacky and in good condition for several months or more.

Cut the puzzle using any of the techniques described earlier. As you approach a figure piece, plan your cutting carefully. While you want the cutting of the figure piece to be successful, you also want the adjoining puzzle pieces to maintain their own visual integrity—that is, they should look similar to the other pieces in the puzzle. As you cut the puzzle, set aside all of the puzzle pieces that have the pattern adhered to them. Once the cutting is completed, remove the bits of paper pattern from the puzzle pieces. Take care when you do this so that you do not tear any of the puzzle picture beneath the pattern. If you use your fingernail, tweezers, or other tool to lift the edge of the pattern, be careful not to scratch the picture.

Some puzzle makers use devices to make the patterns easier to remove. One way to do this is to cut a small V shape in the center of the pattern before applying it to the puzzle. Turn the point of the V up and crease it back to form a tab after removing the backing paper. Adhere the pattern in position on the puzzle board. The V will stand up above the surface, providing a convenient tab by which to remove the pattern from the puzzle piece. Another method is to glue a small (#4) flathead screw to the center of the pattern with Duco cement. After the cement has dried, place the pattern on the puzzle board. The screw is easily gripped to remove the pattern and can be used over and over again.

Signature Pieces

A signature piece is simply a variation of a figure piece that consists of a logo or special figure that the puzzle cutter has adopted as a means of signing a puzzle "in the wood." Two examples of signature pieces are shown, both of which I have used to sign my puzzles. The first signature piece is a monogram with a design based on my initials: EJK. It worked well with strip-cut puzzles but looked out of keeping with free-form puzzles, so I developed a second signature piece based on the outline of a live oak tree. It is the

Signature pieces provide the puzzle maker with an opportunity to sign the puzzle "in the wood." The monogram piece on the left is made from my initials: E.J.K. The logo on the right, an outline of a live oak tree, is used as a trademark for Heritage Puzzles, the name under which I currently market my puzzles.

logo for Heritage Puzzles and is the signature piece I now use for my puzzles. It is intended to signify a well-crafted puzzle destined to be handed down from one generation to the next.

Designing your own signature piece will require much thought and many sketches. When you think you have a good design, try it out on a small plywood square like those used in chapter 2 for learning to cut interlocks. It may be too difficult to cut or too fragile to stand up under the abuse of puzzle assembly. Modify and recut your signature piece until it satisfies both your desire for a unique piece and the complexity of wooden jigsaw puzzle cutting. After you have settled on a design, try cutting some puzzles using the signature piece. Experiment with the placement of the pattern and with the shape of the pieces surrounding it.

Once you adopt a signature piece, you'll be surprised at how people will pore over your puzzles trying to locate it. You also will find it personally satisfying, since as long as the puzzle remains intact, your signature piece will be part of it.

Upside Down and Backward

One other technique that can be used to include figure pieces, signature pieces, and specially designed pieces in a puzzle is to draw a full-size pattern of the puzzle cutting design, adhere it to the back of the puzzle, and cut the puzzle with the

A pattern for cutting a puzzle with figure pieces and other complex puzzle pieces can be adhered to the back of the puzzle board and cut with the saw blade reversed so that the teeth point upward rather than down. This minimizes tear-out on the picture surface of the puzzle.

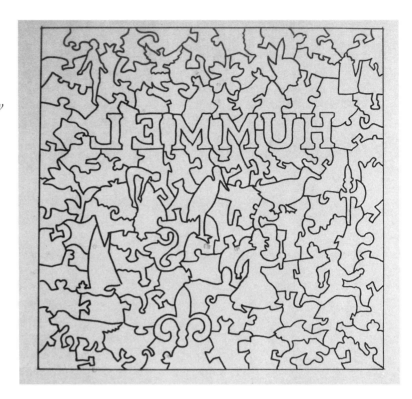

picture face down. The puzzles shown in the accompanying illustrations were cut this way. The first one is a variation on a commercial jigsaw puzzle pattern sold to puzzle cutters in the early 1930s by a printing company.[3] Notice how the name Hummel, the artist whose collage was used for the puzzle image, is placed in the center of the pattern. Notice also that there is little, if any, relationship between the figure pieces and the subject of the puzzle picture—watches. In the second puzzle, which has the same subject, the figure pieces are in the form of gears and escape wheels similar to those used in watch and clock mechanisms, and thus are closely related to the puzzle picture. Keep this in mind when selecting figure pieces, and try, to the extent possible, to relate the figure pieces to the puzzle picture.

The processes used in cutting a puzzle upside down are pretty simple. First, adhere the pattern to the back of a prepared puzzle board using a spray adhesive. Next, cut a piece of drawing or typing paper the same size as the puzzle board, coat it with a repositionable spray

---

3. L. Day Perry and T. K. Webster, Jr., *Jigsaw Puzzles and How to Make 'Em* (Chicago: Mack Publications, 1933), 14.

This jigsaw puzzle, "Watches I," from a collage by William W. Hummel, was cut using the pattern shown in the previous illustration. Note that the figure pieces are unrelated to the subject matter of the puzzle. It measures 10 by 10 3/8 inches and has 130 pieces, including 23 figure pieces.

adhesive, and adhere it to the surface of the picture to protect it during the cutting process. Finally, fasten a blade in the scroll saw upside down—with the teeth pointing away from the saw table. Cut the puzzle following the lines on the pattern. Use a lower speed than usual, and keep a good grip on the puzzle board so that it will not be torn from your hands by the upward pull of the saw blade. After you have finished cutting the puzzle, remove the blade from the saw and reinstall it with the teeth pointing downward. If you forget to do this, you may damage the next puzzle you start to cut.

The paper on the upper surface of the puzzle pieces can be peeled away easily. Be gentle in removing this paper so that you do not accidentally damage the picture. There is a safer, but slower, way to remove the paper from both the front and back of the puzzle pieces: Cut a piece of paper towel to fit in a shallow container such as a margarine tub lid, and pour a small amount of paint thinner on the piece of towel. Then press a puzzle piece into the lid and allow it to soak in the paint thinner for a few seconds. When the pattern has been well dampened with paint thinner, it will peel off easily. Wipe off any adhesive remaining

This pattern of watch gears and escapement is more closely related to the subject matter of the puzzle in the previous illustration.

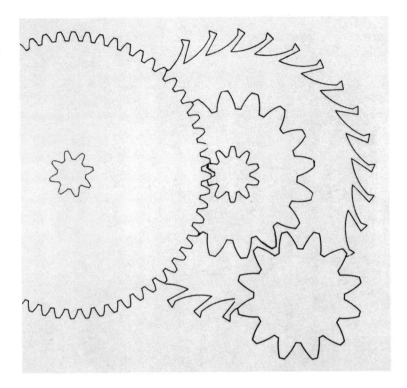

on the wood with a paper towel. Repeat the process for the other side of the puzzle piece. Once the paper has been removed from both surfaces of all of the puzzle pieces, finish the puzzle as described in chapter 2.

Layered Puzzles

A whole new world of wooden jigsaw puzzle making is opened for exploration when you begin making layered puzzles. I was first inspired to develop this kind of puzzle by an antique wooden jigsaw puzzle in the form of an ocean liner. Each layer of the puzzle represented a deck of the ship, with engines, staterooms, gang-

ways, and ladders. The puzzle was held together with thin metal rods that ran through each deck and ended in the form of ventilation pipes.

As the name suggests, layered puzzles are three-dimensional. They are created by placing one puzzle on top of another, each layer held in alignment with the other by special pieces known as *key pieces.*

A key piece consists of a puzzle piece from one layer that is glued to a puzzle piece from the layer directly above it. Each layer is keyed to the layer directly above it. For example, in a three-layered puzzle there would be one set of keys

In this puzzle, "Watches II," you can see the figure pieces of gears and escapement wheels, which in turn have been cut into free-form puzzle pieces. The puzzle, from a collage by William W. Hummel, measures 10 by 10³/8 inches and has 155 pieces, including 5 figure pieces.

connecting the first layer to the second layer and a second set of keys connecting the second layer to the third layer. Each set usually consists of four keys, one for each corner of the puzzle board making up that layer.

Layered puzzles also offer an opportunity to combine images in unusual ways. For example, you can use for the background layer a photograph of a beautiful landscape and for the foreground picture

a photograph of your own house. An interesting feature of layered puzzles is that each layer is a complete puzzle in itself, so one layer can have straight edges and another can have irregular edges.

When you are making a layered puzzle, you'll need to give some thought to what kind of picture should be on each layer. It may be helpful to think of the layers as scenery on a stage, the bottom layer being background, the top layer foreground, and any layers between these two middle ground. The instructions that follow are for a two-layer puzzle but they also apply to puzzles of more than two layers.

Look through your collection of pictures or photographs for likely candidates for the layers. The images need to be approximately the same size and have the same compositional orientation, either horizontal or vertical. Some pictures can be trimmed to the same size without losing any essential details or qualities. If photographs are used, color photocopies can be made to enlarge or

reduce the two images so that they are the same size.

Glue the selected pictures to puzzle boards as described earlier. Do not apply any finish to the back of the puzzle boards, however; a finish would not allow the key pieces to be glued together. Cut the upper puzzle board along the line that you wish to form the irregular edge of the top layer. Set aside that portion of the puzzle board that is not to be used.

Plan the placement of the key pieces in the top layer. There should be four key pieces in all: one in each of the bottom

The picture on this uncut puzzle board will be used as the bottom layer of a three-dimensional, layered puzzle. It is from a photograph of a rural scene in Germany.

The picture above, on an uncut puzzle board, will be used for the top layer of a layered puzzle. It is from a photograph of a village in southwestern England. The illustration below shows the top puzzle board with the sky and fields cut away, leaving only the village scene.

The two layers of the layered puzzle are aligned with one another using key pieces. A key piece consists of a puzzle piece from the bottom layer glued to a puzzle piece from the layer directly above it.

corners and one on each side near or at the top of the puzzle board. Cut each key piece in the top layer so that its interlocks are in the form of sockets (the interlocks extend into the body of the puzzle piece). Later, when you cut the bottom half of the key piece, its inter-

locks will be in the form of knobs that extend outward from the body of the puzzle piece. This arrangement facilitates the assembly of the finished puzzle; the puzzle pieces adjacent to the key pieces in the bottom layer can be more easily identified and put into place. Were the arrangement of interlocks reversed, (the bottom piece having interlocks extending into the body of the puzzle piece) it would be difficult to determine which other puzzle pieces fitted it. In addition, the other pieces would have to be in place before the key piece could be inserted. Replace the key pieces in the puzzle board. Carefully align the top layer on the bottom so that their edges coincide precisely. Remove one of the key pieces and apply a very small drop of

The four key pieces that align the two layers of the puzzle are shown in this illustration. One is in the bottom right corner, another in the bottom left corner, a third near the top of the right side, and the fourth at the top of the left side.

The completed puzzle showing the two layers joined as a single puzzle. This puzzle, "An English Village in a German Setting," measures 10 1/8 by 14 3/8 inches and has a total of 397 pieces in its two layers.

glue to its underside, nearer to the corner than to the interlock sockets. Slip the key piece back in place, being careful not to disturb the alignment of the layers. Press the key piece down and apply firm pressure for several minutes. While still holding the key piece in position, carefully move the rest of the top layer to be certain that it has not become glued to the bottom layer.

Do not disturb the first key piece for at least five minutes to provide time for the glue to set. Make certain the upper board is still precisely aligned with the lower puzzle board, and then glue a second key piece in place in the same manner. Repeat for the third and fourth key pieces.

After all of the key pieces have been glued to the bottom layer, allow the glue several hours to set, and then remove the top puzzle board. Cut the bottom portion of the four key pieces so that the interlocks extend outward from the puzzle piece as described earlier. Leave a

1/16- to 1/8-inch border extending beyond the top part of each key piece. When all four of the key pieces have been cut, both puzzle boards can be cut into pieces. Remember to provide interlocks for all the edge pieces.

Assemble the bottom puzzle and sand its back on the finishing frame. Because of their thickness, the key pieces will have to be sanded separately. Vacuum the puzzle, turn it over, and reinsert the key pieces. Assemble the upper layer, sand its back, and then reassemble it on the bottom layer. The puzzle is finished.

~ *Five* ~

Children's Puzzles

THERE ARE TWO MAJOR DIFFERENCES between children's puzzles and those intended for adults: scale and content. Generally speaking, children's puzzles are smaller and have fewer and larger pieces than adult puzzles. Subject matter in children's puzzles tends to be illustrations of well-known children's stories, poems, and fairy tales. In addition, some children's puzzles are intended to be educational. Keep these differences in mind as you make the transition from adult puzzles to those for children.

Dissected Map Puzzles

You will recall from the Introduction that the earliest known jigsaw puzzle was a wooden dissected puzzle made by John Spilsbury in about 1766. Called "Europe

Divided into Its Kingdoms," it consisted of a map in which the puzzle pieces were formed by cutting along the boundaries of the various countries of Europe. The puzzle was intended to be an educational aid in learning geography.

Dissected puzzles are still popular today, and many elementary schools probably have some. The subject matter for contemporary dissected puzzles ranges from anatomy to biology to geography to technology. There is almost no area of elementary education that cannot be further clarified by the use of dissected puzzles. With this in mind, our first puzzle for children will be a dissected puzzle.

First you need to decide on the subject matter. A map, similar to Spilsbury's, would be challenging to make and interesting to assemble. You would next need to decide what map to use. When the United States consisted wholly of the forty-eight contiguous states, other than some major problems in scale, a map of the country could be easily converted into a jigsaw puzzle. Unless the puzzle is very large, however, the extremely small size of Rhode Island, the two sections of the Delmarva peninsula with parts of Maryland and Virginia, and the panhandle of Maryland between Virginia and Pennsylvania present major cutting problems. With the addition of Hawaii and Alaska, it is difficult to make a dissected puzzle of the country without taking great liberty in the definition of the boundaries of those two states. You can make a map of almost any individual state and cut it along county boundaries without encountering as great a problem with scale. The map can come from a variety of sources; state highway maps prepared by the state department of transportation are public domain, which means they can be used without any copyright infringement. Reduce the map on a photocopier to a size that can be cut on your scroll saw and that also will be a convenient size for children to assemble.

The dissected map puzzle described in the following instructions is a self-contained tray puzzle. Chapter 4 discussed tray puzzles in conjunction with puzzles without interlocks. In a dissected map puzzle, the border of the map will form a frame, which will be glued to a base to create a tray for assembling the puzzle. Self-contained puzzles are very appropriate for use with children, as it helps to prevent the individual pieces from becoming lost. Missing pieces will be apparent immediately.

There was a theorem in geography holding that any map, no matter how complicated, can be colored using only five different colors. Efforts to disprove this theorem have been made in the past, but recently the theorem was proven to be a fact through the use of a complex computer program. Although a map showing geographic features, transportation routes, and major cities would make a perfectly good puzzle, a more interesting and educational one can be made by using a map that simply shows the outlines of the counties, painted in five colors.

The map used in the dissected puzzle shown was made from a black and white photocopy of a map of state game lands in Pennsylvania. The map you select should have a border at least 3/4 inch wide on all four sides. Make two photocopies of it. Trim the map, leaving its border intact, and then measure it. Subtract 1/4 inch from each dimension and cut two pieces of plywood to this size. You may finish the back of one piece of plywood if you wish, but do not apply any finish to either side of the plywood panel to which the map is to be glued.

Apply spray adhesive to the back of the map, move it to a clean, smooth surface, and lower the unfinished puzzle board on

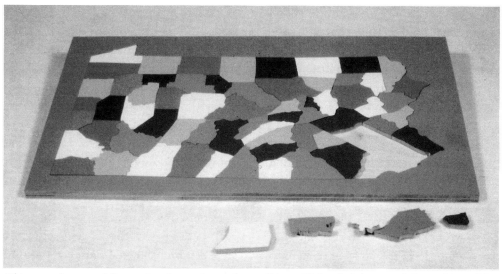

This puzzle map of Pennsylvania continues the tradition of John Spilsbury and the making of dissected jigsaw puzzles. Only five different colors were needed to paint the map, with no two adjacent pieces being the same color. It is a tray puzzle measuring 11 by 18 inches and has 68 pieces.

top of the map, leaving a 1/8-inch border on all sides. Turn the puzzle board right side up and rub the surface of the map to be sure it is firmly affixed to the plywood.

After the map is in place on the puzzle board, follow the directions for tray puzzles in chapter 4 to separate the map from its border. Sand the back and inside edges of the border to remove any splinters or tear-out, then temporarily set the border aside. Cut the map along the borders of the various counties. When cutting out the counties, you'll learn something about geography and politics as you try to figure out why certain county lines seem to follow well-defined geographical features while others seem to have no rhyme nor reason to their shapes.

Assemble the map within the plywood border and sand it as described earlier. Then remove the puzzle pieces and glue the border to the back to form the puzzle tray. Finish the puzzle tray by removing the excess wood from its borders on a table saw, and hand sand the edges to round off sharp corners. Remove any glue on the inside of the tray that may have oozed out from beneath the frame. Use a paper towel dampened with paint thinner to remove the paper map and any adhesive from the puzzle pieces and border.

A wood sealer should be applied to the puzzle, then the counties as well as the border of the map can be painted using nontoxic acrylic paint. Now is your opportunity to see whether the five-color theorem is fact or fiction. Mix five colors of paint that both complement and contrast well with one another. Study the map and determine which county should be painted which color. It's helpful to have a second copy of the map and make a mark on each county to represent the color it should be painted. When you have sorted it out so that no piece of one color is adjacent to another piece of the same color, separate the pieces into five different groups according to color. Apply a coat of spray adhesive to five different pieces of cardboard, each large enough to hold the puzzle pieces of one of the colors. Let the adhesive dry for about five minutes, then place the puzzle pieces for each color on a separate piece of cardboard. The spray adhesive will hold them in place while they are painted.

Important note: Be certain that all paints and finishes are nontoxic and follow manufacturers' instructions.

Pour a small amount of one color of paint in a shallow dish or lid. Dip a small stencil brush into it and use a stippling motion against the bottom of the dish to remove excess paint. Apply the paint to each of the pieces using the same stippling motion. This will give the pieces an even coating but at the same time will prevent the paint from running down the sides of the puzzle pieces. The border could be colored the same as one of the five colors used for painting the counties, but a sixth color probably would provide a more suitable contrast.

Cut the second copy of the map around the borders of the state, and place it in the interior of the puzzle tray as a liner to prevent the tray bottom from being spattered with paint. Paint the border with the sixth color using the same stippling motion. Do not apply any paint to the interior of the puzzle tray. The contrasting color of the plywood with those of the puzzle pieces will assist in the assembly of the puzzle.

When the paint has dried, examine each piece to see that it is evenly covered. You probably will find that a second coat of paint is required. After the second coat of paint has dried, the puzzle is finished and can be assembled. If you make a label for the puzzle (see the next chapter), you may want to place it on the inside of the tray under the puzzle pieces in order to protect it from wear.

"Noah's Ark" Puzzle

The "Noah's Ark" puzzle is similar to the dissected map puzzle in that it is based on the concept of a tray holding the various pieces of the puzzle. It differs, however, in that the puzzle pieces are animals, and the two trays that hold the animals, when closed like a book, represent the ark. It is designed for younger children and has the advantage that the animals can stand alone and thus be used outside of the context of the ark.

At first glance it may appear that this is really not a puzzle because it consists merely of the two halves of the ark with

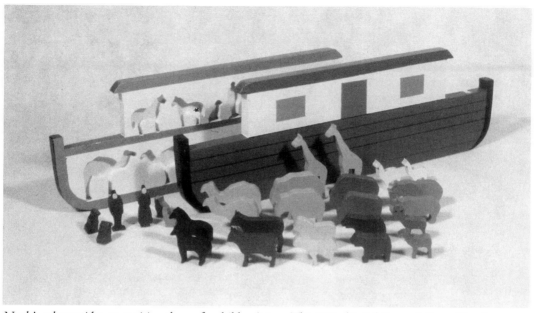

Noah's ark provides an exciting theme for children's toys. This "Noah's Ark" puzzle has niches in the interior of the two halves of the ark, each niche fitted with one animal. The animals also may be played with outside of the context of the ark. The puzzle measures 5¹/2 by 16 inches and holds 28 puzzle pieces in the form of animals as well as Noah and his wife.

niches to hold the various animals. Closer examination will reveal, however, that each animal fits into only one niche. Finding the right niche for each animal is what makes it a puzzle.

The ark, as noted above, is made in two halves. Patterns for the ark are provided at the end of this section. Each half is constructed from three layers of ¹/4-inch plywood. Construction is similar to a tray puzzle in that a border piece is glued to a plywood back. Cut two pieces of ¹/4-inch plywood so that they measure 6 by 18¹/2 inches, with the grain running lengthwise. Temporarily set them aside. Cut four more pieces measuring 6¹/2 by

19 inches. Examine each side of the four pieces and sort them into pairs so that the best side of each panel is on the outside. Glue the two plywood panels in each pair together to form two ¹/2-inch-thick pieces of plywood, using the same process you used when gluing a picture to a puzzle board, but applying glue to both of the plywood surfaces. Although allowance has been made in the plan for errors, keep the two pieces of plywood as accurately aligned as possible when clamping them together. Use clamping cauls to distribute the clamping pressure evenly and to prevent marring the plywood.

In this view, all of the puzzle pieces can be seen fitted into their niches inside the two halves of the ark.

When the glue has set, clean away any glue that may have oozed out from between the pieces of plywood. Examine the long edge of each panel and, if necessary, joint one edge to form a straight edge for sawing. Set the fence of the table saw so that it measures 6 1/4 inches to the closest edge of the saw blade. Place the straight or jointed edge of one of the panels against the fence and rip the panel. Repeat the process with the second panel. Reset the fence of the saw so that it measures exactly 6 inches to the closest edge of the saw blade. Place the sawn edge of one of the panels against

the fence and again trim the piece of plywood. Repeat with the second panel.

Set the miter gauge of the table saw to exactly 90 degrees and square one end of each panel, removing no more than 1/4 inch of wood. Measure 18 1/2 inches from this end, and scribe a line across the other end of each panel. Trim this end of each panel with the table saw and miter gauge. You should now have two 1/2 inch-thick and two 1/4-inch-thick plywood panels 6 inches wide and 18 1/2 inches long.

The plans for the ark are two-thirds scale and will need to be enlarged by 150 percent. This is easily done on most photocopiers. Make photocopies of the plans for both sides of the interior of the ark as well as for the outside of the ark. The exterior and the two interior views of the ark each consist of a bow half and a stern half. These halves will need to be joined together to make the complete full-size plan. When you have completed photocopying each half of each plan, mark the six sheets with the word *master,* preferably in red ink, and then make two more copies of each. Set the masters aside to use should additional copies be required.

Temporarily set aside the patterns for the outside of the ark. Cut the patterns for the interior of the ark on the outside lines. Trim one sheet of each pair along the dotted vertical middle line, and glue the two halves together using rubber cement or a similar adhesive. Use care when joining the two halves to ensure that they are perfectly aligned with one another, with the middle line just showing. Completely coat the back of one of the patterns with spray adhesive, allow it to dry for a few seconds, and then place it on one of the 1/2-inch-thick plywood panels, taking care to accurately align the pattern to the board. Rub the pattern down against the board with the palm of your hand to ensure that it adheres completely. Repeat the process with the second interior pattern.

You will need to drill two 1/16-inch-diameter entry holes through each panel, one for each row of animals. Locate these holes where indicated on the plans. A drill press is recommended for this step to ensure that the holes are drilled perpendicular to the surface of the plywood. This will help in the threading of saw blades and the cutting out of the animals.

Because of the thickness of the plywood panels, you'll need to use a #2 or #3 scroll saw blade to ensure that the openings for the animals are cut perpendicular to the surface. Starting with one of the panels, thread the scroll saw blade through either one of the holes and clamp its upper end as described for making tray puzzles in chapter 4. Set the scroll saw speed to 1,000 SPM or slower, switch on the saw, and begin cutting the first animal. Your objective is to cut around the outer line surrounding the shape of the animal. This will form the niche in which the animal will be stored. When you have cut all the way around the animal and have reached the hole where you began, switch off the saw, remove the animal, and set it aside. Position the plywood panel so that the blade is in front of the line connecting the right foot of the animal just cut with the left foot of the next animal to be cut. Switch the saw back on and follow the line until you reach the outside line just beyond the left foot of the animal to be cut. Cut out the second animal following the same procedure as for the first. Be alert for symptoms of a dull blade, and replace as frequently as necessary. When you have cut all the animals in one row,

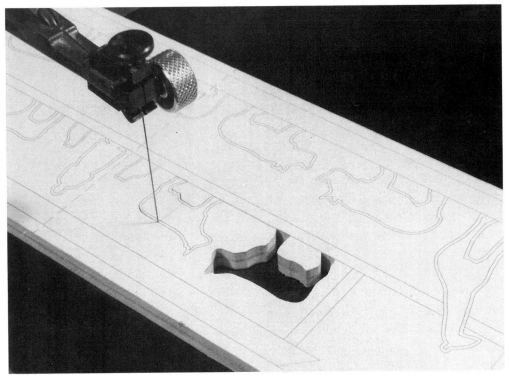

The first step in cutting out the animals is to cut the niches in which they fit. Since this is an interior cut, you have to drill a hole and thread the saw blade through it to cut the first niche, after which you can cut the remaining niches in the same row.

thread the saw blade through the other hole in the panel and cut the second row of animals. Cut the animals from the second plywood panel in the same manner.

Temporarily set the animal pieces aside. Sand the back of each panel to remove all tear-out. Do not, however, remove the paper pattern from the front of the panel; you'll need it later, and it also will serve to remind you which side is to be glued to the backing piece of plywood. Do a trial clamping of each piece using either spring clamps and clamp pads

or C-clamps and cauls. Then spread glue on the back of the interior piece with a small brush, keeping well away from the edges of the animal cutouts. Assemble the two parts, clamp them together, and put aside until the glue has set. Glue the second interior piece to its backing board in the same way.

Replace the large blade in the saw with a #2/0 blade, tension it, and saw around each animal, following the inner line as accurately as possible. Concentrate especially on the small details such as

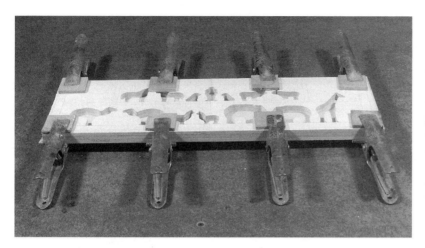

After all of the niches have been cut, the interior portion of each side is glued to a backing board. Here, spring clamps and clamping pads are used to hold the two parts together while the glue sets, although C-clamps and cauls could also be used for this purpose.

horns and hooves. Now peel the paper patterns from the animals. Rub off any adhesive remaining on the surface of the plywood with a piece of paper towel dampened with paint thinner. Sand all of the animals with abrasive paper, rounding and softening all edges except the bottom of the animals' feet. Wrap a quarter sheet of abrasive paper into a flat tube to make a useful tool for getting into curved areas and small places. When you are finished sanding, check to see that each animal can stand on a level surface. If not, level the feet on the sanding board, removing a minimum amount of wood.

When the glue has had time to set, clean out any excess glue from the recesses cut for the animals. Replace the blade in the scroll saw with a #2 or #3 saw blade and cut each panel around the outline of the ark. Remove the remaining paper pattern as described above, and fill the saw slots cut between the feet of the animals in each row with wood filler. Sand the surfaces and edges of the ark to

The outline of each animal is trimmed so that it will have sufficient clearance when it is placed in its niche in the ark.

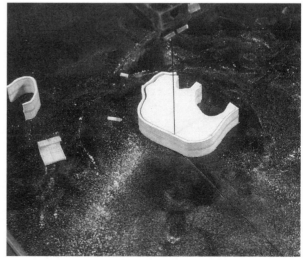

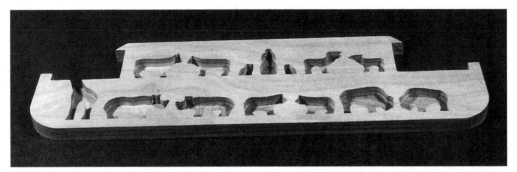

Once the backing board has been glued to the inside portion, each side of the ark is trimmed following the outline of the pattern, after which the pattern is removed.

remove tear-out and splinters. Gently round over the edges, especially around the recesses where the animals fit.

Place each animal in its appropriate space. It should fit in easily, and when the ark half is turned upside down, it should fall out readily. If there is any binding, file and sand the animal until it fits loosely in its space. You'll notice that one of the animals in each pair is smaller than the other. This way, each animal fits in only

one space in the ark, and it also differentiates the male and female animals.

Once all of the animals have been fitted to their spaces, give them a final sanding with abrasive paper. Apply a coat of sealer, and then paint the ark and each of the animals with acrylic paint, following the instructions given for the map puzzle. Select colors for the ark and for the animals that you think are the most appropriate. Again, be certain that all

This view of "Noah's Ark" shows the layout of the outside of the ark. It is used as a guide when painting the ark.

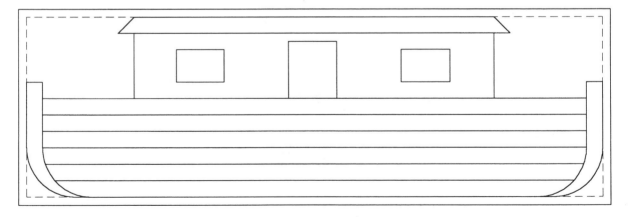

paints and finishes you use are nontoxic. Mix a tablespoon or so of paint for each pair of animals so that you'll have enough of each color to give the animals two or more coats of paint as required. Store leftover paint in margarine tubs or small jars until all the painting has been completed. When the paint has dried, put each animal in its niche, place the right and left ark halves together, and the puzzle is finished.

Scale Plans for "Noah's Ark." The plans for the "Noah's Ark" puzzle are two-thirds scale. To make them full-scale, enlarge by 150 percent. This can be done on most photocopy machines.

The top view shows the placement of animals on the inside of the right half of the ark. Note that the giraffe's head extends above the deck of the ark. The bottom view shows the placement of animals on the inside of the left half of the ark. The second giraffe's head also extends above the deck of the ark. When the two halves of the ark are placed together, the heads of the two giraffes appear side by side above the deck and add a bit of humor to the puzzle.

The dashed line in this plan for the bow half of the right side of the ark indicates where this half is to be joined to the stern half. The plan also shows where holes need to be drilled for inserting the scroll saw blade to cut out the niches for the animals in each row. Enlarge this scale plan, as well as those that follow, on a photocopier by 150 percent.

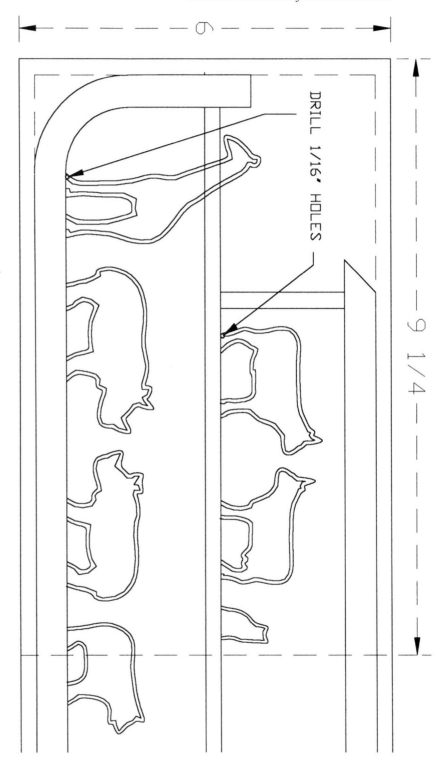

DRILL 1/16" HOLES

9 1/4

The dashed line in this plan for the stern half of the right side of the ark indicates where this half should be aligned and glued to the bow half to form the complete plan for the right side.

The dashed line in this plan for the bow half of the left side of the ark indicates where this half is to be joined to the stern half.

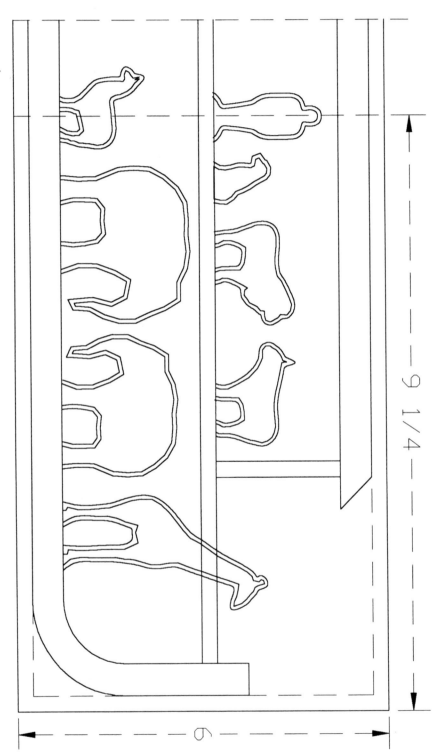

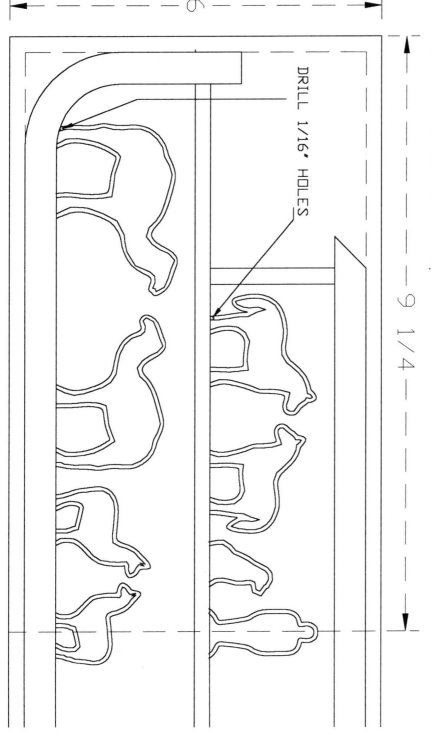

DRILL 1/16" HOLES

The dashed line in this plan for the stern half of the left side of the ark indicates where this half should be aligned and glued to the bow half to form the complete plan for the left side. The plan also shows where holes need to be drilled for inserting the scroll saw blade to cut out the niches for the animals in each row.

The placement of roof, door, and windows on the cabin of the ark, as well as the planking, stem, and stern post, are shown to scale in this plan for the outside bow of the ark. The plan can be used to make patterns as guides for painting the ark. As with the other plans, this one is joined to the stern half at the dashed line.

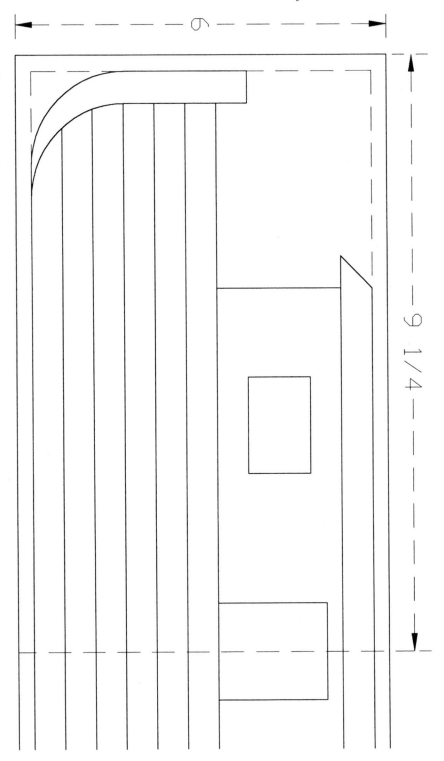

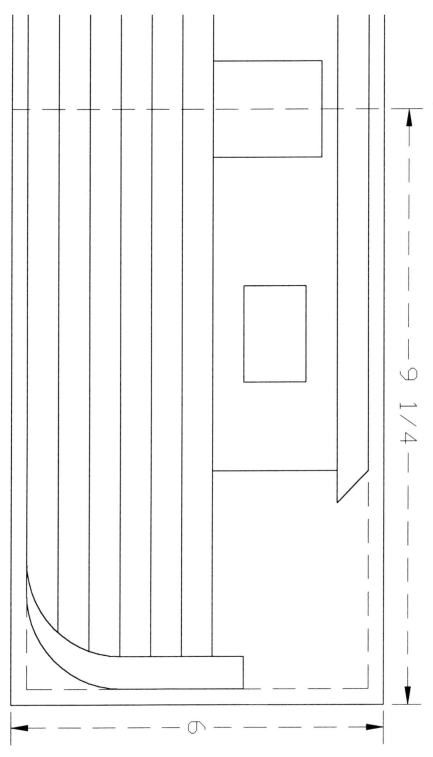

The outside of the stern half of the ark is shown in this plan. It is aligned and glued to the bow half at the dashed line.

9 1/4

6

Storybook Puzzles

The final type of puzzle for children is similar to the layered puzzle described in chapter 4. Here, each layer of the puzzle represents a page in a storybook, a specific action that is central to the tale being told. For example, in the puzzle illustrated, the story of *Goldilocks and the Three Bears* is told using six puzzles that fit one on top of the other. As each layer of the puzzle is assembled, another sequence in the story is told pictorially. The accompanying story is found at the end of this chapter. For now, only the setting of each of the six puzzles will be given, accompanied by a photograph of each of the puzzle boards.

The first puzzle board shows the Three Bears' cottage deep in the forest on a fine spring morning. Goldilocks is standing at the door, and the Three Bears can be seen in the distance walking away from the cottage and into the forest.

The second puzzle board shows an inside view of the cottage. Goldilocks is standing in front of a table on which there are three bowls of porridge. The first is a large bowl, and behind it is a large chair, Father Bear's chair. The second bowl is smaller than Father Bear's bowl, and behind it stands Mother Bear's chair, which is smaller than Father Bear's chair. The third bowl is the smallest of all, and behind it stands Baby Bear's chair.

The tale of Goldilocks and the Three Bears *provides the theme for a complex storybook puzzle with six layers. Each layer relates a major episode in the story. The first layer shows Goldilocks approaching the Bears' cottage as they set off for a walk in the woods while their porridge cools.*

The third puzzle board shows the bedroom in the cottage. There are three beds in the room: a large bed that is Father Bear's, a middle-sized bed that is Mother Bear's, and a small bed that is Baby Bear's. Goldilocks is standing in front of the beds, looking at them, about to test them out.

The fourth puzzle board shows the dining room in the cottage. The Bears are standing in front of the table looking at the bowls of porridge.

The fifth puzzle board shows the bedroom of the cottage. Goldilocks is sleeping on Baby Bear's bed, and the Three Bears are standing in front of the beds looking at Goldilocks.

The sixth puzzle board shows the Three Bears standing on the path outside the cottage door waving to Goldilocks. It is late afternoon, and Goldilocks is walking down the same path she followed coming to the cottage and is waving good-bye to the Three Bears.

To construct a puzzle such as this, you'll need to find a children's story or fairy tale that can easily be told with a few pictures and then find or make appropriate illustrations for the puzzle. You can enlarge or reduce the illustrations as necessary on a color copying machine. All of the pictures should be the same size so that when they are made into puzzles, they will fit on top of one another.

The second layer of the puzzle shows Goldilocks inside the Bears' cottage preparing to sample their porridge.

The third layer shows Goldilocks in the Bears' bedroom looking for a place to take a nap.

The fourth layer shows the Three Bears in their dining room discovering that someone had been eating their porridge.

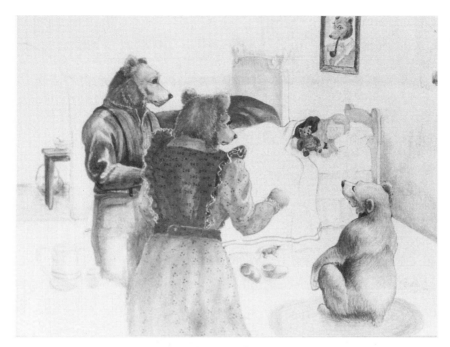

The fifth layer shows the Three Bears in their bedroom finding Goldilocks fast asleep.

The sixth and final layer shows Goldilocks heading down the path for home while the Three Bears wave a friendly good-bye.

Cut pieces of $1/4$-inch plywood to the dimensions of the illustrations in the quantity needed for the story. Sand the edges of each sheet to remove tear-out, and then glue each illustration to a separate panel using the procedures described in chapter 2. Once all the panels have been prepared, stack them in the order in which the story is to be told—that is, with the first illustration on the bottom and the last illustration on top.

Review the processes used for making layered puzzles in chapter 4, and then cut the key pieces in the top layer, placing a key piece at each of the four corners of the puzzle board. Glue the key pieces of the top layer to the puzzle board that is to be directly beneath it. After these key pieces have been cut out, cut the key pieces for the second layer, this time placing them at the midpoint of each of the four sides. In each of the succeeding lay-

This view shows the "Goldilocks" storybook puzzle cut and assembled. It consists of six layers each measuring 7 by 9$1/4$ inches, with a total of 602 pieces. The artwork for each layer was created by Sarah Grant. If your storybook puzzle is intended for young children, you may want to cut larger pieces, perhaps with 50 or fewer pieces to a layer.

ers of the puzzle, alternate the location of the key pieces between the corners and the midpoints, until all the interlocks have been glued in place.

Cut the puzzle boards into pieces, being sure to cut interlocks on all edge pieces. Since this puzzle is intended for a child, you may want to make the puzzle pieces large, perhaps 1 inch square. You may also want to strip-cut the puzzle so that it will not be too complex for a child to assemble; such a puzzle may have more than six hundred pieces. Alternatively, depending on the person for whom the puzzle is intended, you may want to use free-form puzzle pieces and perhaps some figure pieces as well.

Finish each of the puzzles as described in chapter 4. Locate the four key pieces from the bottom layer. Turn them upside down and put a colored dot or other mark on each of them so that the child can use them as clues in assembling the puzzle.

There are, of course, countless other children's puzzles you can make. You just need to use your imagination and apply the various puzzle-making techniques presented in this and other chapters.

***Goldilocks and the Three Bears* Storyline.** When making a storybook puzzle, you'll probably want to include a copy of the story with the puzzle. The story of *Goldilocks and the Three Bears i*s well known, and each version of it tells the story in a slightly different way. The version told here is the one I remember from my childhood.

MOTHER BEAR MADE PORRIDGE FOR BREAKFAST AND POURED IT INTO three bowls on the table. "The porridge is too hot to eat," she said. "Since it's a beautiful spring day, let's take a walk in the forest and pick some flowers while the porridge cools." So Father Bear, Mother Bear, and Baby Bear walked down the trail. As they disappeared into the forest, Goldilocks, who also had been out for a morning walk, came upon the Three Bears' cottage. Since she had walked a long way, she was hungry and tired. She thought to herself, "Perhaps whoever lives here will give me a bite to eat and let me rest for a few moments." So she walked up the path to the cottage door. To her surprise, the door was not latched and it swung wide open when she knocked on it. She waited a few moments and then knocked again. No one answered.

Goldilocks thought, "There must not be anyone home, but since they left their door open, surely they wouldn't mind if I stepped in and rested." She walked into the cottage and saw the table with the three bowls of porridge on it. She thought, "I am so hungry, surely they would not mind if I ate just a little bit of the porridge." She tasted Father Bear's porridge. "Oh! That's too hot!" she cried. Then she tasted Mother Bear's porridge and said, "Yech! That is too cold!" When she tasted Baby Bear's porridge, she exclaimed, "Umm! This is just right!" and she ate it all up.

After eating the porridge, Goldilocks was quite tired, so she looked for a place to take a nap. She opened a door, and there were the Three Bears' beds. There was a large bed for Father Bear, a middle-sized bed for Mother Bear, and a small bed for Baby Bear. Goldilocks tried Father Bear's bed. "Oh! This is too hard!" she cried. She tried Mother Bear's bed and said, "Ugh! This is too soft!" She tried Baby Bear's bed and exclaimed "Umm! This is just right!" and fell fast asleep.

While Goldilocks slept, the Three Bears returned from their walk in the woods and entered the cottage to eat their breakfast porridge. Father Bear growled, "Someone has been eating my porridge!" Mother Bear sighed, "Someone has been eating my porridge!" Baby Bear cried, "Someone has been eating my porridge and ate it all up!" Father Bear said, "I wonder who ate our porridge? Do you suppose they are still in the house?" So the Three Bears started to look for whoever had eaten the porridge.

When they entered the bedroom, Father Bear growled, "Someone has been sleeping in my bed!" Mother Bear sighed, "Someone has been sleeping in my bed!" And Baby Bear cried, "Someone has been sleeping in my bed and there she is!" With that, Goldilocks awakened and saw the Three Bears. She was frightened. Father Bear said, "Don't be frightened, little girl. We won't harm you." "Yes," said Mother Bear, "Don't worry, we are very fond of little girls." Baby Bear said, "Come play with me and be my friend."

Goldilocks and Baby Bear played together all day. They had a wonderful time. Late in the afternoon, Goldilocks decided she should go home before her mother started to worry about her. Baby Bear said, "Please come back and play with me again." Goldilocks promised him that she would, and she set off for home. The Three Bears stood in front of their cottage and waved good-bye as she walked down the path.

Six

Storing and Documenting Puzzles

I N THE PRECEDING CHAPTERS, WE HAVE explored a wide range of wooden jigsaw puzzles. There is almost no limit to their form and subject matter, and with a bit of imagination, you can create almost any kind of puzzle. Now we'll look at how to store and document your finished puzzle.

Storing Puzzles

Except for tray puzzles, which have their own containers, wooden jigsaw puzzles need to be in some kind of container when not in use to keep the puzzle pieces from being lost. Traditionally, puzzles are stored in boxes, although other containers such as cardboard mailing tubes and leather bags have been used.

The box selected for a puzzle should be large enough to easily hold the pieces

of the puzzle, but not so large that the box will seem empty. A wooden jigsaw puzzle when disassembled for storage will occupy about four times its actual volume.[1] For example, a puzzle measuring $1/4$ inch thick, 8 inches wide, and 10 inches long will have a volume of 20 cubic inches (8 x 10 x .25 = 20). Multiplying by 4 shows that we'll need a box that has 80 cubic inches (20 x 4 = 80) of space to store the puzzle. A box that is 2 inches deep, 5 inches wide, and 8 inches long would hold the puzzle. Note that the number of cubic inches is the same as the area in square inches. This is only true if the puzzle is made from $1/4$-inch ply-

---

1. Al Pergande, "Handling Large-Scale Puzzles," *Fine Woodworking* 88 (September-October 1986): 68.

This puzzle has a wooden storage box covered with an enlarged photocopy of the puzzle it contains. The puzzle, "Watches II," was made from a collage by William W. Hummel.

wood, however; if the thickness of the plywood differs from this, you'll have to calculate the volume as above.

Once you know the volume of the box needed for storing your puzzle, you can find a ready-made box of a suitable size for the puzzle or construct your own box. Make sure that the box you choose is sturdy enough to stand up to the wear and tear to which puzzle boxes are subjected.

If you look around your home, you may find a box to fit your puzzle—a note-card box, for example—and you could cover the box with a decorative paper related to the picture puzzle it is to contain. You will soon run out of empty cardboard boxes around the home and even the homes of friends. When this occurs, you can construct your own cardboard boxes. There are paper crafts books available to guide you in this process.

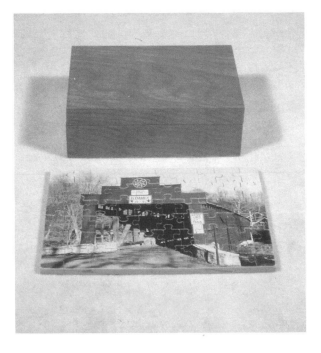

A simple wooden storage box is used for the strip-cut puzzle "Dreibelbis Bridge." The box has been veneered with cherry, a domestic hardwood, and finished with tung oil.

A marquetry crazy-quilt puzzle made with various wood veneers has a matching marquetry storage box.

Wooden boxes are attractive, sturdy, and very appropriate for wooden jigsaw puzzles, since there is a kind of permanence to both. Wooden boxes can be purchased from crafts stores. These boxes usually are plain and unfinished and come in a limited range of sizes. They will need to be painted, varnished, or otherwise decorated to complement your jigsaw puzzle.

You can also make your own wooden box and decorate it in whatever fashion you desire, and thus both the puzzle and the box will be your creations. I construct my boxes from the same 1/4-inch plywood used in making the puzzles they contain, Select Birch, G2S. The construction process is beyond the scope of this book, however.

The two-drawer storage chest for this puzzle is unique in that it repeats the design of the drawers shown in the puzzle it holds. The chest is constructed from mahogany, ebony, and holly. The puzzle, "Studley Tool Chest," is from a poster published by the Taunton Press. It measures 16 1/2 by 16 5/8 inches and has 453 pieces, including 12 figure pieces.

Labeling Puzzles

Each puzzle box should be labeled with the puzzle's title, size, number of pieces, and the name of the puzzle maker. The label can be handwritten, typed, or printed by computer. Office-supply stores carry self-adhesive labels in various sizes, or you can make your own paper label and use an adhesive to affix it to the box. Do not use rubber cement, however, since it will deteriorate over a period of time and the label may become seriously discolored or even fail to adhere to the box.

The label may be placed anywhere on the box—the top, end, bottom, or inside the lid, wherever it seems most appropriate. I prefer the inside of the lid, because there the label is protected from wear and tear and does not detract from the appearance of the box.

You also may wish to include a guide picture—a photograph or other illustration of the puzzle intended to help in assembly. If your puzzle is a reproduction of a work of art, frequently it will be available in both poster size from which to make the puzzle and postcard size from which to make the guide picture. Alterna-

tively, you can use a color photograph or color photocopy of the original picture. Have this made before cutting the puzzle.

Use an adhesive to affix the guide picture to the box. If you use a water-based adhesive such as Elmer's glue, do not get the paper too wet with glue, or it will wrinkle. If you use a spray adhesive, tape the corners of the picture down with masking tape before spraying so

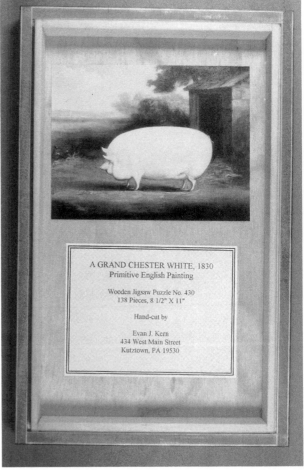

Prepare a guide picture and a label for each boxed puzzle. Here they are shown glued to the underside of the lid of a wooden storage box.

that the picture will not be lifted by the force of the spray, allowing adhesive to get on the front.

Inventorying Puzzles

Many puzzle makers keep a written inventory of their creations in order to keep track of which puzzles have been sold or given away and which remain available as well as to provide a written record for the use of scholars or collectors at some later date. You may feel that it is not worth the effort to maintain an inventory of your puzzles. Should you make more than a few and sell them or give them away, however, at some time in the future they will begin to show up at yard sales and flea markets and begin to be collected by individuals interested in wooden jigsaw puzzles. Eventually someone is going to want to know more about your puzzles, and your written record will be of great help to them.

A puzzle inventory can be kept on paper or on a computer, using an inventory program. I use both systems, filling out an inventory sheet in the studio after each puzzle is cut and then transferring this information to a computer program designed to keep track of the puzzles.

Certain basic information should be recorded in your puzzle inventory:

1. The puzzle number.
2. The title.
3. The dimensions.
4. The number of pieces.
5. The date the puzzle was cut.
6. The disposition of the puzzle.
7. Any comments pertinent to the specific puzzle.

Each of your puzzles should be assigned a number, running in sequence according to the date the puzzles were cut.

In addition to recording the puzzle's width and length (either in fractions or in decimal inches as you prefer) you may want to make a note of the area of the puzzle at the same time. You may find this information useful for several purposes: (1) to determine the size of a container for storing the puzzle pieces, (2) aid in pricing the puzzle if you intend to sell it, and (3) as discussed below, to determine how closely you are approaching some personal standard for the size of puzzle pieces you should cut.

You can determine the number of pieces in a puzzle, if it is a strip-cut puzzle, simply by multiplying the number of strips cut by the number of pieces in each strip. If the puzzle has been cut by some other method, then you will have to count the pieces. One of the easiest ways to do this is during the cleaning process. After cutting, put the pieces into the cleaning screen, hold the screen over the puzzle tray, and shake gently to get rid of most of the sawdust. Then take the pieces from the cleaning screen, count them, and put them into a box or other container. Record the number of pieces on the inventory sheet.

Counting the puzzle pieces also enables you to determine rather accurately the average size of the individual pieces and how close that size comes to some standard you may have set for yourself. For example, if you have been trying to cut puzzles so that the pieces average about $3/4$ inch square, the pieces' area should average approximately .5625 square inches (.75 x .75). Thus, if you have just finished counting the pieces of a puzzle measuring 8 by 10 inches and find that there are 143 pieces, their average area is (8 x 10) ÷ 143, or .5594 square inches, and you have been successful in reaching your goal.

The date the puzzle was cut should be recorded as the date you finish cutting the puzzle, and not when the cutting began. You may begin cutting a puzzle and then put it aside for several days or even weeks before finishing it, and therefore the date you began to cut the puzzle would not be an accurate account of when it actually was cut.

The disposition of the puzzle refers to what finally happened to the puzzle: whether it is in storage, has been sold or given away, or has been discarded. (Yes, sometimes you may actually throw away a puzzle because it does not meet your standards.)

Under comments, record anything distinctive about the puzzle, as for example, the number and kind of figure pieces cut or other information that may prove of value in labeling this specific puzzle or in cutting future puzzles.

Now we have explored almost every facet of making traditional wooden jigsaw puzzles. It's up to you to continue learning and to extend the art of puzzle-making to ever higher levels of interest and complexity. I hope you will take on the challenge.

Seven

Shop-Made Tools and Equipment

~

IN THIS SECTION, PLANS AND INSTRUC-
tions are provided for some of the
tools and equipment you can construct
to assist you in making jigsaw puzzles.
Their construction does not require any
special tools or equipment beyond those
found in most amateur woodworking
shops.

Although you need only a scroll saw
fitted with an appropriate blade to cut
wooden jigsaw puzzles, there are several
accessories that can enhance the cutting
of puzzles. These include an auxiliary saw
table, a saw table for small pieces, and a
tray to hold the puzzle pieces after they
have been cut. Other accessories
included here are designed for use when
gluing up puzzles, for cutting puzzles
with a fretsaw, and for use when finishing
puzzles.

Auxiliary Scroll Saw Table

Many scroll saw tables are made from
aluminum, which functions adequately
for most sawing activities. When cutting
jigsaw puzzles, however, the puzzle board
is turned in many, different directions as
each piece is being cut. As a consequence, some of the aluminum rubs off
the table top and onto the back of the
puzzle board, leaving unsightly gray
marks. This problem can be solved by
making an auxiliary saw table.

The best material from which to construct the auxiliary table is 1/4-inch-thick
tempered hardboard. It is quite dense and
will stand up under extended usage.
Begin by cutting a piece of hardboard 1/2
inch or so larger than the scroll saw table.
Remove the blade from the scroll saw,
and clamp the hardboard to the saw table

so that it extends on all sides. Draw the outline of the saw table with a pencil, including the slot for changing blades, on the underside of the hardboard. Then remove the clamps and hardboard from the saw table.

Fasten a blade to the scroll saw and cut out the auxiliary table. Check it against the saw table to be sure that it fits. Sand the edges and round them off so that there are no sharp corners, especially on the underside, where they could interfere with its fastening to the scroll saw table. It is not necessary to put any kind of finish on the auxiliary table. In fact, as the table is used, a finish would wear off rapidly. Strips of double-faced carpet tape across the back and front edges of the auxiliary table can be used to hold the auxiliary table in place on the saw table. When you want to remove the auxiliary table, gently pry up one corner at the back of the saw table and gradually pull upward until the auxiliary table comes free. Any residue from the tape remaining on the saw table can be removed with paint thinner or a similar solvent.

Saw Table for Small Pieces

When you are cutting very small pieces on the scroll saw, such as the animals for "Noah's Ark," there may be a tendency

The addition of an auxiliary table to scroll saws with aluminum tables will prevent the aluminum from rubbing off onto the back of the puzzle board. It is constructed from hardboard and is held in place with double-sided carpet tape.

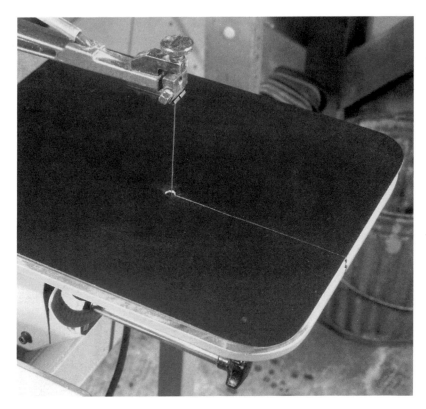

An auxiliary table with only a small hole for the passage of the saw blade is needed when you are cutting small figures, like the animal pieces in the "Noah's Ark" puzzle, to prevent the piece of wood from tipping into the blade recess and binding the scroll saw blade. It is constructed from plastic laminate and is affixed to the auxiliary table with a coat of repositionable adhesive.

for the pieces to tip into the opening for the sawblade and bind. A special saw table for the auxiliary table above will prevent this from happening. A plastic laminate works best, although you can also make the table from a thin sheet of hardboard. The table shown in the accompanying illustration covers only half of the auxiliary table, because that was the size of a scrap of plastic laminate that I had on hand. Its small size has not been a hindrance to its use. This saw table is made the same way as the auxiliary table, except that the hole for the saw blade is made with a 3/16-inch drill bit. Apply a generous coat of repositionable spray

adhesive to the back, and position this table on the top of the auxiliary table when needed. It can be removed easily and set aside when not required.

Scroll Saw Tray Shelf

A shelf fitted to the left side (or the right if you are left-handed) of the top of the scroll saw stand will prove convenient for holding a small cake pan or similar tray in which to store puzzle pieces as they are cut. The design for the tray shelf is shown in the accompanying drawing. The shelf is made of 1/4-inch hardboard or plywood, and the bracket from a piece of 3/4-inch softwood such as pine or spruce.

When you are cutting a jigsaw puzzle, it is convenient to have a tray close at hand to hold the puzzle pieces after they are cut. A small shelf attached to the scroll saw table can be used to hold the tray.

The size of the tray shelf is determined by the size of the tray.

The first step is to measure the top of the saw stand in the area where the tray shelf will be fitted. Using these measurements, lay out the shelf on a piece of hardboard or plywood, allowing sufficient space for the tray and any edgings that may be required. Cut the shelf to size. Try the shelf on top of the saw stand and against the base of the saw where it is to be fastened. Make any adjustments to the shelf that are necessary to fit it to the base of the saw. The shelf should extend perpendicular to the saw stand or to an imaginary centerline of the saw.

Cut a small, triangular bracket from a piece of softwood to fit beneath the shelf and against the side or leg of the saw stand to provide support for the overhang of the shelf. Fasten the bracket to the bottom of the shelf with two #8, 3/4-inch countersunk flathead wood screws so that they are flush with the surface of the shelf.

If the tray is made of steel, strips of magnetic tape with adhesive backing (available at most craft stores) can be applied to the top of the shelf to hold the tray in place. If the tray is made of some nonmagnetic material such as plastic or aluminum, glue 1/4-inch by 3/4-inch strips of wood to the edges of the shelf to keep the tray in place.

Sand the shelf and bracket to remove

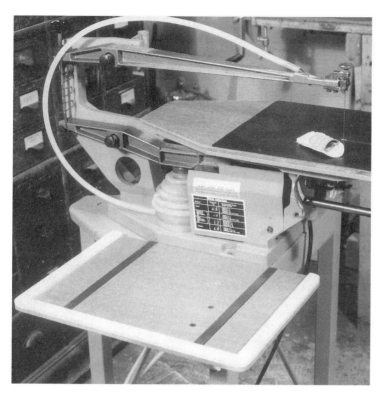

The scroll saw tray shelf is made of hardboard and fastened to the saw table with bolts or screws. A triangular brace between the bottom of the shelf and the frame of the saw table adds rigidity to the shelf. An edging surrounds three sides of the shelf to prevent a nonmagnetic tray from sliding off. Strips of magnetic tape can be used to hold a steel tray.

any splinters or sharp edges. The shelf can be attached to the top of a wooden stand with countersunk flathead wood screws. If the stand is constructed of metal, use countersunk flathead steel stove bolts to hold the shelf in place. You'll need to drill holes through both the shelf and the top of the table saw stand to accommodate the bolts.

Cauls and Caul Supports

Cauls are thick, flat boards used to clamp the glued plywood puzzle board to the puzzle picture. The three pairs of cauls shown in the accompanying drawing will cover the range of sizes of most of the puzzles you'll make. If you wish to glue up puzzles larger than the 12-by-18-inch caul shown, you may have difficulty applying sufficient pressure over the entire surface of the puzzle board. When this occurs, the paper may not completely adhere in some areas or wrinkles may appear in the glued surface. Consequently, if you wish to make larger puzzle boards, you should use a different means of clamping, such as a vacuum press, which consists of a special plastic bag connected by a hose to a vacuum pump. The glued puzzle board and picture are placed between cauls and the whole assembly is placed in the bag. When the air is evacuated from the bag with the vacuum pump, the weight of the atmosphere creates a pressure of about 10 pounds per square inch, evenly distributed over the surface of the puzzle board. An 8-by-10-inch puzzle would have a pressure of 800 pounds on it, more than adequate for gluing the picture to the puzzle board. You can find instructions for making a vacuum press in woodworking books and magazines. A vacuum press is ideal for gluing pictures to puzzle boards for it assures a smooth, wrinkle-free picture surface.

The cauls should be made from 3/4-inch-thick plywood or multidensity fiber board. Their surfaces should be perfectly even, and a pair of cauls should fit tightly together with no apparent gaps. Sand the top and bottom surfaces of the cauls absolutely smooth and round all sharp edges and corners to prevent injury to

you or damage to the puzzle picture. Give the cauls two coats of varnish or tung oil to prevent glue from adhering to them. After the finish has completely dried, give both surfaces of each caul a coat of paste wax for added protection.

You'll need a pair of caul supports for each set of cauls. Unless you plan to use more than one pair of cauls at a time, however, only four support strips are needed to cover the entire range of cauls, because the length of one set of cauls is the same as the width of the next set. The supports are made from 1/4-inch plywood to the dimensions given. The width of the support strips will be determined by the distance your C-clamps overhang a piece of wood when tightened. Add about 1/4-inch to this distance, and use this measurement when cutting

The various sizes of cauls, as well as an assembled caul support, are shown in this illustration. The additional sections of supports shown can be used to expand the range of cauls they can hold.

the strips of plywood for the caul supports. Set the fence of the table saw to this measurement and cut all the strips at once, to ensure that they are all the same width. Cut the four strips to the length given in the plans, and then use the table saw to cut the slots by which the support strips are joined to one another. The slots should be cut so that they are barely wider than the thickness of the plywood and slightly more than half the width of the strip. This will enable them to fit together easily and to lie flat on the surface of the workbench. The edges of the strips should be sanded to remove splinters, but there is no need to apply any finish. Do not glue the pieces together, since they can be used to make different size stands as needed.

You will need sufficient 3-inch C-clamps so that when they are spaced around the periphery of the cauls, they will be 4 to 6 inches apart. For the largest puzzle boards, you also will need at least two deep-throated clamps that will reach to the center of the caul so that pressure can be applied there as well.

Fretsaw Table

The fretsaw table shown is used in conjunction with the fretsaw for cutting wooden jigsaw puzzles, as described in chapter 3. It is clamped to the top of the workbench and can be removed and stored when not in use. It is designed so that the V-shaped notch, or bird's mouth, in the table extends beyond the edge of the workbench. This provides the clear-

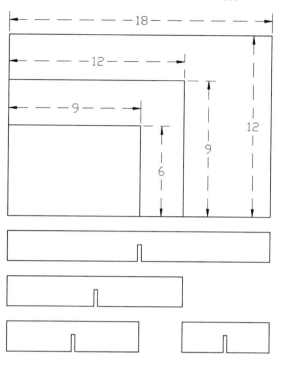

When gluing a picture to a puzzle board, smooth-surfaced clamping cauls are needed to prevent the puzzle from wrinkling as the glue sets. The range of cauls shown will cover most puzzle-making needs. The caul supports, shown at the bottom, are helpful in holding the cauls above the surface of the workbench when placing the C-clamps in position around the outer edges of the cauls.

ance needed for the hand and the saw when the table is being used.

The fretsaw table should be constructed from 3/4-inch hardwood plywood or hardwood lumber, depending on what is available, and consists of three parts: a table with a V-shaped notch, a raising block, and a base for clamping the saw table to the workbench. Simple butt joints are employed throughout, and glue and screws are used to fasten the parts together. The only critical dimension is the width of the raising block, which needs to be high enough so that the saw table is a convenient height when cutting with the fretsaw. This height will depend on the height of your workbench and the height of the chair or stool you are using. If you sit when you use your scroll saw, make the height of the fretsaw table the same as the height of the table on your scroll saw. The raising block also will have to be high enough so that the bottom of the puzzle board will clear the tops of the clamps used to secure the table to the workbench.

Check to be certain the blade of the table saw is at 90 degrees to the table; then cut the pieces to the dimensions given on the plans. Mark the centerline and lay out the V notch on the top side

of the piece forming the table. The notch may be cut on the scroll saw, since no great degree of accuracy is required. Mark the location of the screw holes on the centerline, and drill clearance holes for #8-by-1 1/2-inch, flathead steel wood screws using a #19 drill bit. Drill all holes on a drill press, if possible, to ensure that they are perpendicular to the surface of the wood. Countersink the holes so that the heads of the wood screws will be slightly below the surface of the table. Turn the table over and mark where the raising block is fastened. Extend the lines forward and to the sides of the block's position, as well as up the back edge of the table. These lines will be used to align the raising block when you drill the holes for the lead screws.

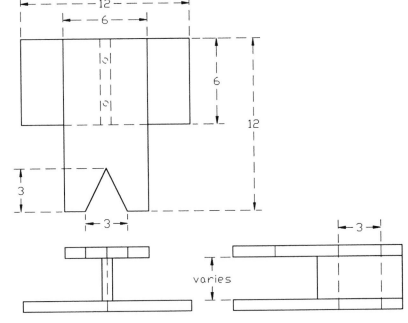

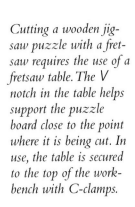

Cutting a wooden jig-saw puzzle with a fret-saw requires the use of a fretsaw table. The V notch in the table helps support the puzzle board close to the point where it is being cut. In use, the table is secured to the top of the work-bench with C-clamps.

Write the word *table* on one long edge of the raising block, and the word *base* on the opposite edge. Draw a centerline the length of both the top and the bottom of the raising block. Measure the position of the lead hole for the screw closest to the rear edge of the saw table. Drill a lead hole 1 inch deep using a #42 drill bit.

Clamp the raising block in a wood vise with the table side uppermost and the top edge clear of the jaws of the vise. Insert one of the wood screws into the hole nearest the edge of the table, and push it through so that its point extends slightly from the underside of the board. Align the point of the screw with the hole in the raising block, and draw the two together with a screwdriver. As you tighten the screw, move the table in whatever direction required to align the raising block with the marks on the underside of the table. Clamp the table and raising block in a wood vise with the V notch facing upward and the top of the table facing the front of the workbench. The head of the screw just inserted should be well below the edges of the vise while the uppermost hole remains clear of the jaws.

Tighten the vise, being certain the table and raising block remain in correct relation to one another. Insert one of the wood screws in the upper hole, and push it in until you can feel the point resting on the top edge of the raising block. Turn the screw several times with the screwdriver to mark the position of the second

lead hole in the raising block. Then remove the assembly from the vise and unscrew the table from the raising block. Drill the lead hole in the raising block, and then repeat the process of assembly just described. This time, however, you also will be able to fasten the table and raising block together with the second screw.

Again, separate the table from the raising block and repeat the above procedures, this time marking out and joining the raising block to the clamping base with wood screws. Stagger the location of the screws so that they will not run into the screws holding the top to the raising block. When this has been accomplished, rejoin the table to the top of the raising block, and check the entire assembly to be sure all parts fit as they should. Since this is not a precision process, do not be concerned with minor errors in alignment. The essential point is that both the table and the base should draw up tight against the raising block.

When you are satisfied with the fit of the three pieces, disassemble the fretsaw table one last time, and apply glue to the top edge of the raising block and the bottom of the table where the raising block fits. Join the two together with the wood screws, pulling the screws up tight. Wipe away any excess glue. Repeat the process and join the clamping base to the bottom edge of the raising block. The fretsaw table can be used as soon as the glue has set.

Cleaning Screen

The cleaning screen is a convenient tool for getting rid of the sawdust from cutting and sanding that clings to the individual puzzle pieces. The cleaning screen consists of 1/4-inch hardware cloth stretched across a wooden frame. Directions and measurements for the screen are given in the accompanying plan.

The frame is constructed from 3/4-inch lumber. Almost any softwood or hardwood will do. Joint one edge of the lumber and then, using a table saw, rip enough strips to the width shown in the plan to construct the sides of the frame. Lower the blade of the table saw until it extends 1/2 inch above the saw table. Set the fence to 1/4 inch and cut a groove the length of each strip. This slot will be used to hold the hardware cloth in place in the frame.

Set the miter gauge of the saw to 45 degrees. Test the accuracy of the setting by cutting some trial pieces of wood to this angle and checking them

with a square. When satisfied with the setting, cut the four sides of the frame to the length shown on the plan. Be certain to cut the miter so that the slot cut for the hardwood cloth will be on the inside.

Measure the length of the groove in one of the frame sides. Subtract 1/4 inch from this measurement, and use tin snips to cut a square piece of 1/4-inch mesh hardware cloth with sides of this length. Cut the hardware cloth so that the ends of the wires extend as little as possible. This will help you when you need to slide the hardware cloth into the frame. Do a trial clamping of the cleaning frame

The cleaning screen consists of a wooden frame with a hardware cloth screen on one side. It is used for cleaning sawdust and sanding dust from the puzzle pieces. A screw eye in the middle of one side of the frame provides a means for hanging the cleaning screen out of the way when not in use.

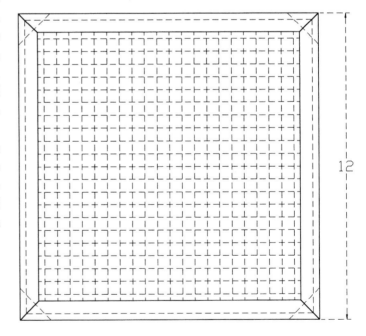

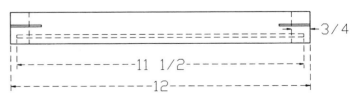

with the hardware cloth seated in the groove in the sides. A picture-framing clamp is ideal for this task, but any other clamping method can be used. When you're satisfied with the fit of the corners and the hardware cloth, remove the frame from the clamps. Remove the hardware cloth and set it aside. Apply glue to two of the joints, and reclamp the frame with the fourth, unglued side in place to ensure that the frame remains square. After the glue in these two joints has had sufficient time to set (at least a half hour), remove the frame from the clamps, insert the hardware cloth into the grooves in the frame, trial fit the fourth side, and when satisfied with the fit, glue and clamp the last two corners.

Once the glue has set, saw a groove $1/2$ inch deep across each corner as shown in the plans to receive a reinforcing slip of wood. The saw cut should be spaced so that it falls at the midpoint of the corner of the frame. Rip a $3/4$-inch-thick piece of wood to the thickness of these saw slots. It should be a firm but not tight fit. Cut four pieces of this strip of wood so that they are about $1/2$ inch longer than the slots, and glue one into each corner slot.

After the glue on the reinforcing strips has set, saw or sand them flush with the edges of the frame. Sand all edges of the cleaning screen frame so that there are no sharp edges or corners. Make sure the bottom edges are well rounded to prevent damage to the puzzle. You do not need to apply a finish to it. Drill a small pilot hole at the midpoint of one side of the screen, and thread a screw eye into it so that you can hang the screen out of the way when it is not being used.

Finishing Frame and Puzzle Hold-Down

The finishing frame provides a means for securely holding a puzzle when sanding its back. It consists of a base made from $1/4$-inch-thick hardboard or plywood. This base has $1/4$-by-$3/4$-inch strips glued to two edges. The frame can be any size desired; indeed, it's useful to have several different sizes.

The construction of the frame is quite easy. Simply cut the material selected for the base to the desired size on the table saw. Rip a strip of plywood $3/4$ inch wide and of sufficient length to make the two edge strips. Cut the strips to length using a simple butt joint where they meet in one corner. Apply glue to one side of one strip and clamp it to the base using spring clamps. Wipe away any excess glue. When the glue has set, remove the clamps and glue the second strip in place. Sand the edges of the finishing frame to remove any splinters. Drill a hole $1/4$ inch in diameter $1/2$ inch from the edge in the middle of one of the sides so that you can hang the frame out of the way when not in use.

Complete the construction of the finishing frame by making a plywood hold-down. Saw it to the width and length shown on the plan, and then use the scroll saw to cut a 90-degree V notch in one end.

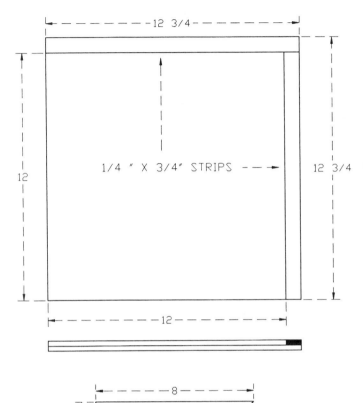

The finishing frame and hold-down provide a convenient way of holding the puzzle securely while you sand the back after it has been cut. In use, the assembled puzzle is turned upside down and slid into the corner formed by the two raised strips on the top of the finishing frame. The hold-down is pressed against the opposite corner of the puzzle and keeps the pieces together. The finishing frame works best with puzzles having inter-locking edges.

of sandpaper around the bottom and sides of the block and hold in place with the hand while sanding.

A sanding board is used to square the edges of puzzle boards, for sanding the backs of puzzle pieces, and for numerous other sanding tasks in the workshop. Make the sanding board from a 12-by-18-inch piece of 1/4-inch-thick hardboard or plywood. Draw a 9- by 11-inch rectangle in the center of the board. Give the back of a sheet of #100-grit abrasive paper a generous coating of spray adhesive, allow to dry a few seconds, and then place within the marked rectangle on the plywood, pressing it down firmly against the wood, especially around the edges. When the abrasive paper becomes worn or clogged, simply peel it off and glue a new sheet in its place.

Sanding Block and Board

A sanding block is an essential tool for sanding the backs of puzzle boards after they have been cut. It is designed to use quarter sheets of abrasive paper and can be made out of any kind of wood. It measures 4 1/2 inches long, 3 inches wide, and 3/4 inch thick with a 1/4-inch-thick pad of dense foam or felt glued to the bottom. This padding enables the sanding block to conform to variations in the surface being sanded. To use, wrap a piece

Sources of Tools and Supplies for Puzzle Making

Advanced Machinery Imports, Ltd.
P.O. Box 312
New Castle, DE 19720-0312
(800) 220-4264
(scroll saws, saw blades, plywood)

Albert Constantine and Son, Inc.
2050 Eastchester Road
Bronx, NY 10461-2297
(800) 223-8087
(fretsaws, saw blades, glues, plywood)

RB Industries, Inc.
1801 Vine St., P.O. Box 369
Harrisonville, MO 64701
(800) 487-2623
(scroll saws, saw blades, plywood)

Trend-lines
135 American Legion Highway
Revere, MA 02151-9117
(800) 767-9999
(scroll saws, saw blades, glues)

Woodcraft
210 Wood County Industrial Park
P.O. Box 1686
Parkersburg, WV 26102-1686
(800) 225-1153
(fretsaws, scroll saws, saw blades, glues)

Woodworker's Supply, Inc.
1108 North Glenn Road
Casper, WY 82601
(800) 645-9292
(fretsaws, scroll saws, saw blades, glues)

REFERENCES

Malavolta, Steve. "Jigsaw Puzzles." *Fine Woodworking* 60 (September–October 1986): 66–69.

Pergande, Al. "Handling Large-Scale Puzzles." *Fine Woodworking* 88 (May–June 1991): 53.

Perry, L. Day, and T. K. Webster, Jr. *Jigsaw Puzzles and How to Make 'Em*. Chicago: Mack Publications, 1933.

Williams, Anne D. *Jigsaw Puzzles: An Illustrated History and Price Guide*. Radnor, PA: Wallace-Homestead Book Co., 1990.

——— "Jigsaw Puzzles: Pictures on Plywood and Scroll Sawn to Pieces." *Fine Woodworking* 88 (May–June 1991): 52–55.